HOLT

Biology
Lab Manual for
Quick Labs, Data Labs,
and Math Labs

P9-CEW-330

HOLT, RINEHART AND WINSTON

A Harcourt Education Company

Orlando • **Austin** • New York • San Diego • Toronto • London

Copyright © by Holt, Rinehart and Winston.

All rights reserved. No part of this publication may be reproduced or transmitted in any form or by any means, electronic or mechanical, including photocopy, recording, or any information storage and retrieval system, without permission in writing from the publisher.

Teachers using HOLT BIOLOGY may photocopy complete pages in sufficient quantities for classroom use only and not for resale.

Printed in the United States of America

ISBN 0-03-074079-7

1 2 3 4 5   054   06 05 04 03

Contents

Copyright © by Holt, Rinehart and Winston. All rights reserved.

Mendel and Heredity

DNA: The Genetic Material

How Proteins Are Made

Gene Technology

History of Life on Earth

Copyright © by Holt, Rinehart and Winston. All rights reserved.

The Theory of Evolution

Quick Lab

Math Lab

Classification of Organisms

Quick Lab

Data Lab

Data Lab

Populations

Quick Lab

Math Lab

Ecosystems

Quick Lab

Quick Lab

Biological Communities

Data Lab

Data Lab

Quick Lab

The Environment

Quick Lab

Copyright © by Holt, Rinehart and Winston. All rights reserved.

Introduction to the Kingdoms of Life

Quick Lab

Protists

Quick Lab

Data Lab

Fungi

Quick Lab

Data Lab

Introduction to Plants

Quick Lab

Data Lab

Quick Lab

Plant Reproduction

Quick Lab

Quick Lab

Quick Lab

Plant Structure and Function

Quick Lab

Quick Lab

Data Lab

Copyright © by Holt, Rinehart and Winston. All rights reserved.

Plant Growth and Development

Introduction to Animals

Simple Invertebrates

Mollusks and Annelids

Arthropods

Copyright © by Holt, Rinehart and Winston. All rights reserved.

Echinoderms and Invertebrate Chordates

Data Lab

Introduction to Vertebrates

Data Lab

Fishes and Amphibians

Data Lab

Reptiles and Birds

Data Lab

Mammals

Quick Lab

Animal Behavior

Quick Lab

Copyright © by Holt, Rinehart and Winston. All rights reserved.

Circulatory and Respiratory Systems

Quick Lab

Math Lab

Quick Lab

Digestive and Excretory Systems

Quick Lab

The Body's Defenses

Quick Lab

Data Lab

Nervous System

Data Lab

Quick Lab

Hormones and the Endrocrine System

Math Lab

Reproduction and Development

Data Lab

Copyright © by Holt, Rinehart and Winston. All rights reserved.

Name _____ Class _____ Date _____

Determining the pH of Common Substances

You can use pH indicator paper to determine the pH of various solutions. The pH indicator paper changes color when it is exposed to a solution. The change in color indicates how acidic or basic the solution is.

MATERIALS

- paper
- pencil
- wide-range pH paper
- three different solutions
- beaker or small jar
- water

Procedure

1. Use the data table below.

2. Predict the pH (acid or base) of each solution, and record your predictions in the data table.

Data Table		
Solution	**Predicted pH**	**Measured pH**

3. Test each solution with pH paper, and record the results in the appropriate row in the data table.

Analysis

1. **Summarize** your findings in two sentences.

_____

_____

_____

_____

_____

Copyright © by Holt, Rinehart and Winston. All rights reserved.

Determining the pH of Common Substances *continued*

2. Determine whether the predictions that you made were correct. Explain any differences between your predictions and your results.

_____

_____

_____

3. Compare your results with those of the rest of the class. Explain any differences.

_____

_____

_____

4. List the steps of scientific methods that you followed while doing this activity.

_____

_____

Copyright © by Holt, Rinehart and Winston. All rights reserved.

Name _____ Class _____ Date _____

DATASHEET FOR IN-TEXT LAB

Analyzing Experimental Design

Background

To study the effects of common substances on the heart rate of a tiny aquatic organism known as *Daphnia*, students placed a *Daphnia* in a drop of water on a glass slide. The students then added 1 or more drops of a test substance dissolved in water to the slide, waited 10 seconds, then counted heart beats for 10 seconds. The students used a clean slide and a new *Daphnia* each time. Their data table is shown below.

Heart Rate of *Daphnia* in Different Solutions	
Substance tested	**Heart rate (beats per minute)**
None (control)	58
Coffee	65
Ethanol	50

Analysis

1. Identify the dependent and independent variables in the experiment.

_____

_____

2. Identify the experimental groups in the experiment.

_____

_____

3. Propose a liquid that could be used for a control group.

_____

4. Evaluate how the instructions could be changed to improve the design of the experiment.

_____

_____

_____

_____

Copyright © by Holt, Rinehart and Winston. All rights reserved.

| Analyzing Experimental Design *continued*

5. Critical Thinking
Applying Information Design an experiment that students can perform to verify the prediction that coffee will increase heart rate in *Daphnia*.

_____

_____

_____

_____

_____

Copyright © by Holt, Rinehart and Winston. All rights reserved.

Name _____ Class _____ Date _____

Analyzing the Effect of pH on Enzyme Activity

Background

The graph shows the relationship between pH and the activity of two digestive enzymes, pepsin and trypsin. Pepsin works in the stomach, while trypsin works in the small intestine. Use the graph to answer the following questions.

Enzymes and pH

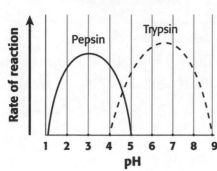

Analysis

1. **Name** the enzyme that works best in highly acidic environments.

_____

2. **Name** the enzyme that works best in less-acidic environments.

_____

3. **Critical Thinking**
   Analyzing Data Identify the pH value at which trypsin works best.

_____

4. **Critical Thinking**
   Analyzing Data Identify the pH value at which pepsin works best.

_____

5. **Critical Thinking**
   Inferring Relationships What does the graph indicate about the relative acidity of the stomach and small intestine?

_____

_____

_____

_____

Copyright © by Holt, Rinehart and Winston. All rights reserved.

Calculating Surface Area and Volume

Background

You can improve your understanding of the relationship between a cell's surface area and its volume by practicing with a large cube with a side length of 4 mm.

1. Find the total surface area of the cube.

- side length (l) = 4 mm
- surface area of one side = $l \times l = l^2$
- surface area of one side (l^2) = 4 mm $\times$ 4 mm = 16 mm^2
- total surface area = $6 \times l^2$ = 6 $\times$ 16 mm^2 = 96 mm^2

2. Calculate the volume of the cube.

- height (h) = l = 4 mm
- volume = $l^2 \times h$ = 16 mm^2 $\times$ 4 mm = 64 mm^3

3. Determine the surface area-to-volume ratio. A ratio compares two numbers by dividing one number by the other. A ratio can be expressed in three ways:

in words	as a fraction	with a colon
x to y	$\dfrac{x}{y}$	$x{:}y$

For the surface are-to-volume ratio, divide total surface area by volume.

$$\frac{\text{total surface area}}{\text{volume}} = \frac{96}{64}$$

Divide both numbers by their greatest common factor:

$$\frac{(96 \div 32)}{(64 \div 32)} = \frac{3}{2}$$

Copyright © by Holt, Rinehart and Winston. All rights reserved.

| Calculating Surface Area and Volume *continued*

Analysis

1. **Calculate** the surface area-to-volume ratio of a cube with a side length of 2 mm.

   _____

   _____

   _____

2. **Calculate** the surface area-to-volume ratio of a cube with a side length of 1 mm.

   _____

   _____

   _____

3. **Critical Thinking**
   Relating Concepts How does the flatness of a single-celled *Paramecium* affect the cell's surface area-to-volume ratio?

   _____

   _____

   _____

   _____

Copyright © by Holt, Rinehart and Winston. All rights reserved.

Name _____ Class _____ Date _____

Observing Osmosis

You can observe the movement of water into or out of a grape under different conditions.

MATERIALS

- 3 grapes
- 3 small jars with lids
- saturated sugar solution
- grape juice
- tap water
- marking pen
- paper towel
- balance

Procedure

1. You will be using the data table below to record your data.

Data Table			
Solution	**Original Mass**	**Predicted Mass**	**Actual Mass**
Sugar solution			
Grape juice			
Water			

2. Fill one jar with the sugar solution. Fill a second jar with grape juice. (The grape will be more visible inside the jar if you fill the jar with white grape juice.) Fill the third jar with tap water. Label each jar according to the solution it contains.

3. Using the balance, find the mass of each grape. Place one grape in each jar, and record the mass of each jar in the data table. Put a lid on each jar.

4. Predict whether the mass of each grape will increase or decrease over time. Explain your predictions.

5. After 24 hours, remove each grape from its jar, and dry it gently with a paper towel. Using the balance, find its mass again. Record your results.

6. Clean up your materials before leaving the lab.

Copyright © by Holt, Rinehart and Winston. All rights reserved.

| Observing Osmosis *continued*

Analysis

1. Identify the solutions in which osmosis occurred.

_____

_____

_____

_____

_____

2. Critical Thinking
Evaluating Conclusions How did you determine whether osmosis occurred in each of the three solutions?

_____

_____

_____

_____

3. Critical Thinking
Evaluating Hypotheses Did the mass of each grape change as you predicted? Why or why not?

_____

_____

_____

_____

_____

Copyright © by Holt, Rinehart and Winston. All rights reserved.

Data Lab

Analyzing the Effect of Electrical Charge on Ion Transport

Background

The electrical charge of an ion affects the diffusion of the ion across the cell membrane. Some ions are more concentrated inside cells, and some ions are more concentrated outside cells. Use the table to answer the following questions:

Ion Charges and Concentration Inside and Outside Cell		
Ion	Charge of ion	Concentration of ion outside cell : inside cell
Sodium (Na^+)	Positive	10:1
Potassium (K^+)	Positive	1:20
Calcium (Ca^{2+})	Positive	10,000:1
Chloride (Cl^-)	Negative	12:1

Analysis

1. **Identify** the ion that is more concentrated inside the cell than outside the cell.

_____

2. **Identify** those ions that are more concentrated outside the cell than inside the cell.

_____

3. **Critical Thinking**
   Recognizing Relationships Do the positive charges of calcium ions and sodium ions make these ions more likely to move into or out of the cell?

_____

_____

4. **Critical Thinking**
   Inferring Relationships Which ions' electrical charges oppose the direction of movement that is caused by their concentration gradient?

_____

_____

_____

_____

_____

Copyright © by Holt, Rinehart and Winston. All rights reserved.

Quick Lab

Identifying a Product of Photosynthesis

You can use the following procedure to identify the gas given off by a photosynthetic organism.

MATERIALS

- MBL or CBL system with appropriate software
- test tube or small glass jar
- sprig of *Elodea*
- distilled water
- cool light source
- dissolved oxygen (DO) probe

Procedure

1. Set up an MBL/CBL system to collect and graph data from a dissolved oxygen probe at 30-second intervals for 60 data points. Calibrate the DO probe.

2. Place a sprig of *Elodea* in a test tube or glass jar, and fill the test tube or jar with distilled water.

3. Place the test tube or glass jar under a cool light source, and lower a DO probe into the water. Collect data for 30 minutes.

4. When data collection is complete, view the graph of your data. If possible, print the graph. Otherwise, sketch the graph on paper.

Analysis

1. **Infer** the cause of any change you observed.

_____

_____

2. **Propose** a control for this experiment.

_____

_____

3. **Critical Thinking**
Evaluating Hypotheses Explain how your data support or do not support the hypothesis that photosynthetic organisms give off oxygen.

_____

_____

Copyright © by Holt, Rinehart and Winston. All rights reserved.

Name _____ Class _____ Date _____

Quick Lab

Modeling Chromosomal Mutations

You can use paper and a pencil to model the ways in which chromosome structure can change.

MATERIALS

- 14 note-card pieces
- pencils
- tape

Procedure

1. Write the numbers 1–8 on note-card pieces (one number per piece). Tape the pieces together in numerical order to model a chromosome with eight genes.

2. Use the "chromosome" you made to model the four alterations in chromosome structure illustrated below. For example, remove the number 3 and reconnect the remaining chromosome pieces to represent a deletion.

3. Reconstruct the original chromosome before modeling a duplication, an inversion, and a translocation. Use the extra note-card pieces to make the additional numbers you need.

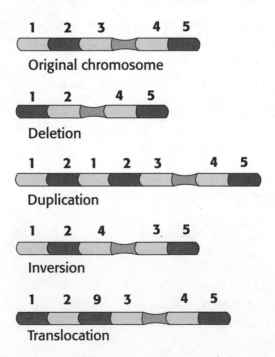

1 2 3 4 5
Original chromosome

1 2 4 5
Deletion

1 2 1 2 3 4 5
Duplication

1 2 4 3 5
Inversion

1 2 9 3 4 5
Translocation

Copyright © by Holt, Rinehart and Winston. All rights reserved.

Modeling Chromosomal Mutations *continued*

Analysis

Describe how a cell might be affected by each mutation if the cell were to receive a chromosome with that mutation.

_____

_____

_____

_____

_____

_____

_____

Copyright © by Holt, Rinehart and Winston. All rights reserved.

Math Lab) **DATASHEET FOR IN-TEXT LAB**

Calculating the Number of Cells Resulting from Mitosis

Background

Scientists investigating cancer might need to know the number of cells produced in a certain amount of time. In the human body the rate of mitosis is about 25 million (2.5×10^7) cells produced every second! You can calculate the number of cells produced by mitosis in a given amount of time.

1. **Calculate the number of cells produced by mitosis in the given time.** For example, to find the number of cells produced in 3 minutes, determine how many seconds there are in 3 minutes (since the rate is given in seconds).

$$\frac{60 \text{ seconds}}{1 \text{ minute}} \times 3 \text{ minutes} = 180 \text{ seconds}$$

2. **Multiply the rate of mitosis by the time (in seconds) asked for in the problem (180 seconds).**

$$\frac{2.5 \times 10^7 \text{ cells}}{\text{second}} \times 180 \text{ seconds} = 4.5 \times 10^9 \text{ cells } (4,500,000,000 \text{ cells})$$

Analysis

1. **Calculate** the number of cells that would be produced in 1 hour.

_____

2. **Calculate** the number of cells that would be produced in 1 day.

_____

3. **Critical Thinking**
Predicting Patterns Identify factors that might increase or decrease the rate of mitosis.

_____

_____

_____

Copyright © by Holt, Rinehart and Winston. All rights reserved.

Observing Mitosis and Cytokinesis

You can identify the stages of mitosis and the process of cytokinesis by observing slides of tissues undergoing mitosis using a compound microscope.

MATERIALS

- compound microscope
- prepared slide of mitosis
- paper
- pencil

Procedure

1. View a prepared slide of cells undergoing mitosis under low power of a compound microscope.

2. Move the slide until you find a section where different stages of mitosis are visible.

3. Switch to high power. Use photos or diagrams from your textbook to help you locate and identify cells in interphase and in each stage of mitosis.

4. On a separate piece of paper, sketch an example of each stage. Label each sketch with the following terms where appropriate: *chromosomes, cell membrane, cytoplasm, nucleus, spindle,* and *cell wall.*

5. Switch to low power, and estimate how many cells are clearly in interphase and how many cells are in one of the stages of mitosis.

Analysis

1. **Describe** the activity of chromosomes in each stage of mitosis.

_____

_____

_____

_____

_____

2. **Compare** the number of cells in interphase with the number of cells in one of the stages of mitosis.

_____

_____

_____

Copyright © by Holt, Rinehart and Winston. All rights reserved.

Observing Mitosis and Cytokinesis *continued*

3. Critical Thinking
Inferring Relationships What does your answer to item 2 indicate about the relative length of interphase?

_____

_____

Copyright © by Holt, Rinehart and Winston. All rights reserved.

Modeling Crossing-Over

You can use paper strips and pencils to model the process of crossing-over.

Homologous chromosomes

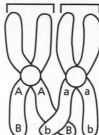

MATERIALS
- 4 paper strips
- pens or pencils (two colors)
- scissors
- tape

Procedure

1. Using one color, write the letters *A* and *B* on two paper strips. These two strips will represent one of the two homologous chromosomes shown above.

2. Using a second color, write the letters *a* and *b* on two paper strips. These two strips will represent the second homologous chromosome shown above.

3. ◆ Use your chromosome models, scissors, and tape to demonstrate crossing-over between the chromatids of two homologous chromosomes.

Analysis

1. **Determine** what the letters *A*, *B*, *a*, and *b* represent.

   _____

2. **Infer** why the chromosomes you made are homologous.

   _____

   _____

3. **Compare** the number of different types of chromatids (combinations of *A*, *B*, *a*, and *b*) before crossing-over with the number after crossing-over.

   _____

   _____

4. **Critical Thinking**
   Applying Information How does crossing-over relate to genetic recombination?

   _____

   _____

Copyright © by Holt, Rinehart and Winston. All rights reserved.

Name _____ Class _____ Date _____

Observing Reproduction in Yeast

Yeast are unicellular organisms that live in liquid or moist environments. You can examine a culture of yeast to observe one of the types of reproduction that yeast can undergo.

MATERIALS

- microscope
- microscope slides
- dropper
- culture of yeast

Procedure

1. Make a wet mount of a drop of yeast culture.

2. Observe the yeast with a compound microscope under low power.

3. Look for yeast that appear to be in "pairs."

4. Observe the pairs under high power, and then make drawings of your observations.

Analysis

1. Infer the type of reproduction you observed when the yeast appeared to be in pairs.

_____

_____

2. Identify the reason for your answer.

_____

_____

_____

3. Determine, by referring to your textbook, the name of the type of reproduction you observed.

_____

_____

Copyright © by Holt, Rinehart and Winston. All rights reserved.

(Math Lab)
Calculating Mendel's Ratios

Background

You can calculate the ratios Mendel obtained in the F_2 generation for the traits he studied.

Data Table			
Contrasting traits	**F_2 generation results**		**Ratio**
Flower color	705 purple	224 white	3.15:1
Seed color	6,022 yellow	2,001 green	
Seed shape	5,474 round	1,850 wrinkled	
Pod color	428 green	152 yellow	
Pod shape	882 round	299 constricted	
Flower position	651 axial	207 top	
Plant height	787 tall	277 dwarf	

Analysis

1. Calculate the ratio for each contrasting trait to complete the table above. Use colon form.

_____

_____

2. State the ratio for each contrasting trait in words and as a fraction.

_____

_____

_____

_____

_____

_____

3. Critical Thinking
Interpreting Results Do the data confirm a 3:1 ratio in the F_2 generation for each of the traits he studied?

_____

Copyright © by Holt, Rinehart and Winston. All rights reserved.

DATASHEET FOR IN-TEXT LAB

Identifying Dominant or Recessive Traits

You can determine some of the genotypes and all of the phenotypes for human traits that are inherited as simple dominant or recessive traits.

MATERIALS

• pencil

• paper

Data Table	
Dominant trait	**Recessive trait**
Cleft chin	No cleft
Dimples	No dimples
Hair above knuckles	Hairless fingers
Freckles	No freckles

Procedure

1. Look at the table above. For each trait, circle the phenotype that best matches your own phenotype.

2. Determine how many students in your class share your phenotype by recording your results in a table on the chalkboard.

Analysis

1. **Summarize** the class results for each trait.

_____

_____

2. **Calculate** the class dominant:recessive ratio for each trait.

_____

_____

3. **Critical Thinking**
   Applying Information For which phenotypes in the table can you determine a person's genotype without ever having seen his or her parents? Explain.

_____

_____

_____

Copyright © by Holt, Rinehart and Winston. All rights reserved.

Data Lab

Analyzing a Test Cross

Background

You can use a test cross to determine whether a plant with purple flowers is heterozygous (*Pp*) or homozygous dominant (*PP*). Fill in the boxes in each Punnett square shown below.

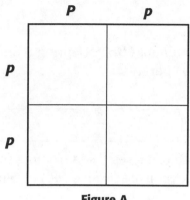

Figure A
Heterozygous (*Pp*) plant

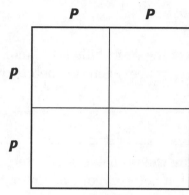

Figure B
Homozygous (*PP*) plant

Analysis

1. Determine what the letters at the top and side of each box represent.

_____

2. Determine what the letters in each box represent.

_____

3. Calculate the genotypic and phenotypic ratios that would be predicted if the parent of the unknown genotype were homozygous for the trait (Figure B).

_____

_____

4. Critical Thinking
Predicting Outcomes If half of the offspring have white flowers, what is the genotype of the plant with purple flowers?

_____

Copyright © by Holt, Rinehart and Winston. All rights reserved.

Math Lab)   **DATASHEET FOR IN-TEXT LAB**

Predicting the Results of Crosses Using Probabilities

Background

In rabbits, the allele B for black hair is dominant over the allele b for brown hair. You can practice using probabilities to predict the outcome of genetic crosses by completing the genetic problems below. Draw Punnett squares for each problem.

Analysis

1. Calculate the probability of homozygous dominant (*BB*) offspring resulting from a cross between two heterozygous (*Bb*) parents.

_____

_____

2. Calculate the probability of heterozygous offspring resulting from a cross between a heterozygous parent and a homozygous recessive (*bb*) parent.

_____

_____

3. Calculate the probability of heterozygous offspring resulting from a cross between a homozygous dominant parent and a homozygous recessive parent.

_____

_____

4. Calculate the probability of homozygous dominant offspring resulting from a cross between a heterozygous parent and a homozygous recessive parent.

_____

_____

Copyright © by Holt, Rinehart and Winston. All rights reserved.

Name _____ Class _____ Date _____

Evaluating a Pedigree

Background
Pedigrees, such as the one below, can be used to track different genetic traits. Use the pedigree below to practice interpreting a pedigree.

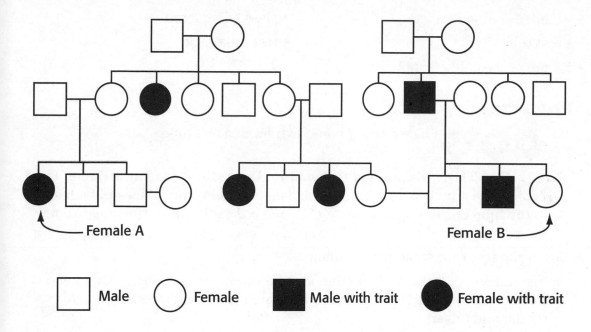

☐ Male   ○ Female   ■ Male with trait   ● Female with trait

Analysis
1. **Interpret** the pedigree to determine whether the trait is sex-linked or autosomal and whether the trait is inherited in a dominant or recessive manner.

   _____

2. **Determine** whether Female A is homozygous or heterozygous.

   _____

3. **Critical Thinking**
   Applying Information If Female B has children with a homozygous individual, what is the probability that the children will be heterozygous?

   _____

Copyright © by Holt, Rinehart and Winston. All rights reserved.
23

DATASHEET FOR IN-TEXT LAB

Observing Properties of DNA

You can extract DNA from onion cells using ethanol and a stirring rod.

MATERIALS

- safety goggles and plastic gloves
- plastic pipet
- 5 mL of onion extract
- glass stirring rod
- test tube
- test tube rack
- 5 mL of ice-cold ethanol

Procedure

1. Place 5 mL of onion extract in a test tube.

2. **CAUTION: Ethanol is flammable. Do not use it near a flame.** Hold the test tube at a 45° angle. Use a pipet to add 5 mL of ice-cold ethanol to the tube one drop at a time. *NOTE: Allow the ethanol to run slowly down the side of the tube so that it forms a distinct layer.*

3. Let the test tube stand for 2–3 minutes.

4. Insert a glass stirring rod into the boundary between the onion extract and ethanol. Gently twirl the stirring rod by rolling the handle between your thumb and finger.

5. Remove the stirring rod from the liquids, and examine any material that has stuck to it. Touch the material to the lip of the test tube, and observe how the material acts as you try to remove it.

6. Clean up your materials and wash your hands before leaving the lab.

Analysis

1. **Describe** any material that stuck to the stirring rod.

   _____

2. **Relate** the characteristics of your sample to the structural characteristics of DNA.

   _____

3. **Propose** a way to determine if the material on the stirring rod is DNA.

   _____

   _____

Copyright © by Holt, Rinehart and Winston. All rights reserved.

| **Decoding the Genetic Code** *continued*

3. Critical Thinking

Recognizing Patterns Determine the sequence of nucleotides in the segment of DNA from which the mRNA strand on the previous page was transcribed.

_____

4. Critical Thinking

Recognizing Patterns Determine the sequence of nucleotides in the segment of DNA that is complementary to the DNA segment described in item 3.

_____

Copyright © by Holt, Rinehart and Winston. All rights reserved.

Name _____ Class _____ Date _____

Modeling Introns and Exons

You can use masking tape to represent introns and exons.

MATERIALS

- masking tape
- pens or pencils (two colors)
- metric ruler
- scissors

Procedure

1. Place a 15–20 cm strip of masking tape on your desk. The tape represents a gene.

2. Use two colors to write the words *appropriately joined* on the tape exactly as shown in the example. Space the letters so that they take up the entire length of the strip of tape. The segments in one color represent introns; those in the other color represent exons.

appropriately joined

3. Lift the tape. Working from left to right, cut apart the groups of letters written in the same color. Stick the pieces of tape to your desk as you cut them, making two strips according to color and joining the pieces in their original order.

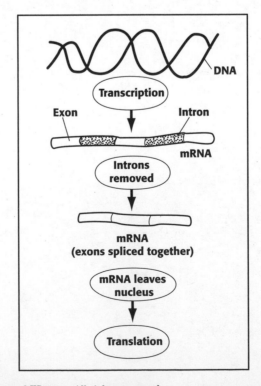

Copyright © by Holt, Rinehart and Winston. All rights reserved.

| Modeling Introns and Exons *continued*

Analysis

1. Determine from the resulting two strips which strip is made of "introns" and which is made of "exons."

_____

_____

2. Critical Thinking

Predicting Outcomes Predict what might happen to a protein if an intron were not removed.

_____

_____

_____

_____

_____

Copyright © by Holt, Rinehart and Winston. All rights reserved.

Name _____ Class _____ Date _____

Modeling Gel Electrophoresis

You can use beads to model how DNA fragments are separated in a gel during electrophoresis.

MATERIALS

- 500 mL beaker
- large jar
- 3 sets of beads—each set a different size and different color

Procedure

1. Fill a large jar with the largest beads. The filled jar represents a gel.

2. Mix the two smaller beads in the beaker and then pour them slowly on top of the "gel." The two smaller size beads represent DNA fragments of different sizes.

3. Observe the flow of the beads through the "gel." Lightly agitate the jar if the beads do not flow easily.

Analysis

1. **Identify** which beads flowed through the "gel" the fastest.

_____

2. **Relate** the sizes of the beads to the sizes of DNA fragments.

_____

_____

3. **Determine** whether the top or the bottom of the jar represents the side of the gel with the positively charged pole.

_____

_____

_____

4. **Critical Thinking**
   Forming Conclusions Why do the beads you identified in Analysis question 1 pass through the "gel" more quickly?

_____

_____

_____

Copyright © by Holt, Rinehart and Winston. All rights reserved.

32

Quick Lab

Modeling Radioactive Decay

You can use some dried corn, a box, and a watch to make a model of radioactive decay that will show you how scientists measure the age of objects.

MATERIALS

- approximately 100 dry corn kernels per group
- cardboard box
- clock or watch with a second hand

Procedure

1. Assign one member of your team to keep time.

2. Place 100 dry corn kernels into a box.

3. Shake the box gently from side to side for 10 seconds.

4. Keep the box still and remove and count the kernels that "point" to the left side of the box. Record in the data table below the number of kernels you removed.

Data Table		
Total shake time (seconds)	**Number of kernels removed**	**Number of kernels remaining**
10		
20		
30		
40		
50		
60		

5. Repeat steps 4 and 5 until all kernels have been counted and removed.

6. Calculate the number of kernels remaining for each time interval.

7. Make a graph using your group's data. Plot "Total shake time (seconds)" on the x-axis. Plot "Number of kernels remaining" on the y-axis. Use a separate sheet of graph paper.

Copyright © by Holt, Rinehart and Winston. All rights reserved.

| Modeling Radioactive Decay *continued*

Analysis

1. Identify what the removed kernels represent in each step.

_____

_____

2. Calculate the half-life of your sample, in seconds, that is represented in this activity.

3. Calculate the age of your sample, in years, if each 10-second interval represents 5,700 years.

4. Evaluate the ability of this model to demonstrate radioactive decay.

_____

_____

_____

_____

_____

Copyright © by Holt, Rinehart and Winston. All rights reserved.

Modeling Coacervates

By using simple chemistry, you will see that some properties of coacervates resemble the properties of cells.

MATERIALS

- safety goggles and lab apron
- graduated cylinder
- 1 percent gelatin solution
- 1 percent gum arabic solution
- test tube
- 0.1 M HCl
- pipet
- microscope slide and coverslip
- microscope

Procedure

1.   **CAUTION: Hydrochloric acid is corrosive. Put on safety goggles, gloves, and a lab apron. Avoid contact with skin and eyes. Avoid breathing vapors. If any of this solution spills on you, immediately flush the area with water, and notify your teacher.**

2. Mix 5 mL of a 1 percent gelatin solution with 3 mL of a 1 percent gum arabic solution in a test tube.

3.   Add 0.1 M HCl to the gelatin-gum arabic solution one drop at a time until the solution turns cloudy.

4. Prepare a wet mount of the cloudy solution, and examine it under a microscope at high power.

5. Prepare a drawing of the structures that you see.

Copyright © by Holt, Rinehart and Winston. All rights reserved.

Modeling Coacervates *continued*

Analysis

1. **Describe** what happened to the solutions after the acid was added.

   _____

   _____

2. **Compare** the appearance of coacervates with that of cells.

   _____

   _____

   _____

   _____

3. **Predict** what would happen to the coacervates if a base was added to
   the solution.

   _____

   _____

   _____

   _____

4. **Critical Thinking**
   Evaluating Hypotheses Based on the evidence you obtained, defend the
   hypothesis that coacervates could have been the basis of life on Earth

   _____

   _____

   _____

   _____

   _____

Copyright © by Holt, Rinehart and Winston. All rights reserved.

Data Lab

Analyzing Signs of Endosymbiosis

Background

You may recall that mitochondria have their own DNA and produce their own proteins. The data below were collected by scientists studying the proteins produced by mitochondrial DNA. The scientists found that the three-nucleotide sequences (codons) in the nucleus of an organism's cells can code for different amino acids than those coded for in the cell's mitochondria. Examine the data below, and answer the questions that follow.

Amino Acids Made in the Nucleus and Mitochondria			
	Amino acids or other instructions coded for in the nucleus	Amino acids or other instructions coded for in mitochondria	
Codon	Plants and mammals	Plants	Mammals
UGA	Stop	Stop	Tryptophan
AGA	Arginine	Arginine	Stop
AUA	Isoleucine	Isoleucine	Methionine
AUU	Isoleucine	Isoleucine	Methionine
CUA	Leucine	Leucine	Leucine

Analysis

1. **Defend** the theory of endosymbiosis using these data.

_____

_____

_____

2. **Infer** what these data indicate about the evolution of plant cells.

_____

_____

_____

3. **Describe** how these data can be used to support the idea that more than one type of cell evolved early in the history of life.

_____

_____

_____

Copyright © by Holt, Rinehart and Winston. All rights reserved.

Name _____ Class _____ Date _____

Modeling Natural Selection

By making a simple model of natural selection, you can begin to understand how natural selection changes a population.

MATERIALS

- paper
- pencil
- watch or stopwatch

Procedure

1. You will be using the data table provided to record your data.

2. Write each of the following words on separate pieces of paper: *live, die, reproduce, mutate.* Fold each piece of paper in half twice so that you cannot see the words. Shuffle your folded pieces of paper.

3. Exchange two of your pieces of paper with those of a classmate. Make as many exchanges with additional classmates as you can in 30 seconds. Mix your pieces of paper between each exchange you make.

4. Look at your pieces of paper. If you have two pieces that say "die" or two pieces that say "mutate," then sit down. If you do not, then you are a "survivor." Record your results in the data table.

Data Table			
Student name	**Trial 1**	**Trial 2**	**Trial 3**

Copyright © by Holt, Rinehart and Winston. All rights reserved.

Modeling Natural Selection *continued*

5. If you are a "survivor," record the words you are holding in the data table. Then refold your pieces of paper and repeat steps 2 and 3 two more times with other "survivors."

Analysis

1. **Identify** what the four slips of paper represent.

_____

_____

_____

2. **Describe** what happens to most mutations in this model.

_____

_____

_____

3. **Identify** what factor(s) determined who "survived." Explain.

_____

_____

_____

4. **Evaluate** the shortcomings of this model of natural selection.

_____

_____

_____

Copyright © by Holt, Rinehart and Winston. All rights reserved.

Name _____ Class _____ Date _____

DATASHEET FOR IN-TEXT LAB

Analyzing Change in Lizard Populations

Background

In 1991, Jonathan Losos, an American scientist, measured hind-limb length of lizards from several islands and the average perch diameter of the island plants. The lizards were descended from a common population 20 years earlier, and the islands had different kinds of plants on which the lizards perched. Examine the graph and answer the questions that follow.

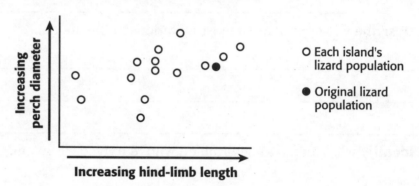

Hind-Limb Length Variation

Analysis

1. **Interpreting Graphics** How did the average hind-limb length of each island's lizard population change from that of the original population?

_____

_____

2. **Predict** what would happen to a population of lizards with short hind limbs if they were placed on an island with a larger average perch diameter than from where they came.

_____

_____

3. **Justify** the argument that this experiment supports the theory of evolution by natural selection.

_____

_____

_____

_____

_____

Copyright © by Holt, Rinehart and Winston. All rights reserved.

Quick Lab

Using a Field Guide

You can use a standard pictoral field guide or a dichotomous key to help you identify species of plants, animals, or other organisms.

MATERIALS

• paper and pencil

• a plant or an animal field guide

Procedure

1. ⚠ **CAUTION: Wear protective gloves when handling any wild plant. Keep your hands away from your face.** Using a dichotomous key or other field guide, identify several species of plants that share the same phylum and class. Collect specimens only if your teacher tells you to do so.

2. Try to identify two plants of the same genus.

3. Record the scientific name of each specimen in the table below.

Specimen	Genus name	Binomial species name	Identifying characteristics
A			
B			
C			

4. Read the description of each species in the field guide. Determine the set of characteristics that fit each specimen. Write these characteristics in the table.

Analysis

1. **List** the characteristics shared by two specimens that are in the same genus but are different species.

_____

_____

2. **Describe** how the binomial names of these two species show that they are members of the same genus.

_____

_____

Copyright © by Holt, Rinehart and Winston. All rights reserved.

Using a Field Guide *continued*

3. Identify the key characteristics your field guide uses to tell these two
species apart.

_____

_____

4. Critical Thinking
Analyzing Data Based on your observations, are two species from the same
genus more similar or less similar than two species from different genera?

_____

_____

Copyright © by Holt, Rinehart and Winston. All rights reserved.

Data Lab

Analyzing Taxonomy of Mythical Organisms

Background

Classification of organisms often requires grouping organisms based on their characteristics. Use the following list of mythological organisms and their characteristics to complete the analysis.

- **Pegasus** stands 6 ft tall, has a horse's body, a horse's head, four legs, and two wings.

- **Centaur** stands 6 ft tall, has a horse's body with a human torso, a male human head, and four legs.

- **Griffin** stands 4–6 ft tall, has a lion's body, an eagle's head, four legs, two wings, fur on its body, and feathers on its head and wings.

- **Dragon** can grow to several hundred feet, has a snake-like body, from 1 to 3 reptile-like heads, four legs, scales, and breathes fire.

- **Chimera** stands 6 ft tall, has a goat's body, snake's tail, four legs, a lion's head, fur on its body and head, scales on its tail, and breathes fire.

- **Hydra** is several hundred feet long, has a long body with four legs and a spiked tail, 100 snake heads, scales, and is poisonous.

Analysis

1. **Identify** the characteristics that you think are the most useful for grouping the organisms into separate groups.

   _____

   _____

2. **Classify** the organisms into at least three groups based on the characteristics you think are most important.

   _____

   _____

   _____

3. **Evaluate** the use of the biological species concept to classify these mythical organisms.

   _____

   _____

   _____

Copyright © by Holt, Rinehart and Winston. All rights reserved.

Data Lab

Making a Cladogram

Background

A cladogram is a model that represents a hypothesis about the order in which organisms evolved from a common ancestor. Scientists construct a cladogram by first analyzing characters in a data table. The absence of a vascular system and the absence of seeds is ancestral. Use the data below to construct a cladogram on a separate sheet of paper.

Characters		
Plants	**Seeds**	**Vascular system**
Horsetails	No	Yes
Liverworts	No	No
Pine trees	Yes	Yes

Analysis

1. Identify the out-group.

_____

_____

2. Name the least common derived character.

_____

_____

3. List the order in which the plants in the table would be placed on a cladogram.

_____

_____

Copyright © by Holt, Rinehart and Winston. All rights reserved.

Quick Lab

Demonstrating the Hardy-Weinberg Principle

You can model the allele frequencies in a population with this simple exercise.

MATERIALS

- equal numbers of cards marked *A* or *a* to represent the dominant and recessive alleles for a trait
- paper bag

Procedure

1. You will be using the data table provided to record your data.
2. Work in a group, which will represent a population. Count the individuals in your group, and obtain that number of both *A* and *a* cards.
3. Place the cards in a paper bag, and mix them. Have each individual draw two cards, which represent a genotype. Record the genotype and phenotype in your data table.

Data Table

	Trial 1	Trial 2	Trial 3	Trial 4	Trial 5
Genotype					
Phenotype					

4. Randomly exchange one "allele" with another individual in your group. Record the resulting genotypes.
5. Repeat Step 4 four more times.

Analysis

1. **Determine** the genotype and phenotype ratios in your group for each trial. Do the ratios vary among the trials?

_____

_____

_____

2. **Hypothesize** what could cause a change in the "genetic makeup" of your group? Test one of your hypotheses.

_____

_____

_____

_____

Copyright © by Holt, Rinehart and Winston. All rights reserved.

Math Lab   **DATASHEET FOR IN-TEXT LAB**

Building a Normal Distribution Curve

Background

You can help your class build a normal distribution curve by measuring the length of your shoes and plotting the data.

MATERIALS

- paper
- pencil
- measuring tape
- graph paper

Procedure

1. You will be using the data table provided to record your data.

2. Measure and record the length of one of your shoes to the nearest centimeter. Record your measurement and your gender.

Data Table

Shoe length (cm)	Gender	Shoe length (cm)	Gender

3. Formulate a hypothesis about whether female shoes as a group are longer, shorter, or the same as shoes from males.

4. Determine the number of shoes of each length represented in the class.

5. Using a sheet of graph paper, make a graph showing the distribution of shoe length in your class. Show the number of students on the y-axis and shoe length on the x-axis.

6. Make a second graph using data only from females.

7. Make a third graph using data only from males.

Copyright © by Holt, Rinehart and Winston. All rights reserved.

Analysis

1. Describe the shape of the curve that resulted from the graph you made in step 5.

_____

_____

2. Distinguish how the distribution curve for shoe length of females differs from the curve for the shoe length of males.

_____

_____

_____

3. Predict how the distribution curve that you made in step 5 would change if the data for males was deleted.

_____

_____

Copyright © by Holt, Rinehart and Winston. All rights reserved.

Name _____ Class _____ Date _____

Evaluating Biodiversity

By making simple observations, you can draw some conclusions about
biodiversity in an ecosystem.

MATERIALS

- note pad
- pencil

Procedure

1. **CAUTION: Do not approach or touch any wild animals. Do
   not disturb plants.** Prepare a list of biotic and abiotic factors that
   you observe around your home or in a nearby park.

Analysis

1. **Identify** the habitat and community that you observed.

   _____

2. **Calculate** the number of different species as a percentage of the total number
   of organisms that you saw.

   _____

   _____

3. **Rank** the importance of biotic factors within the ecosystem you observed.

   _____

   _____

   _____

4. **Infer** what the relationships are between biotic factors and abiotic factors in
   the observed ecosystem.

   _____

   _____

   _____

   _____

   _____

   _____

Copyright © by Holt, Rinehart and Winston. All rights reserved.

Modeling Succession

You can create a small ecosystem and measure how organisms modify their environment.

MATERIALS

- 1 qt glass jar with a lid
- one-half quart of pasteurized milk
- pH strips

Procedure

1. You will be using the data table below to record your data.

Data Table		
Day	**pH**	**Appearance**
1		
2		
3		
4		
5		
6		
7		

2. Half fill a quart jar with pasteurized milk, and cover the jar loosely with a lid. Measure and record the pH. Place the jar in a 37°C incubator.

3. Check and record the pH of the milk with pH strips every day for seven days. As milk spoils, its pH changes. Different populations of microorganisms become established, alter substances in the milk, and then die off when conditions no longer favor their survival.

4. Record any visible changes in the milk each day.

Copyright © by Holt, Rinehart and Winston. All rights reserved.

Modeling Succession *continued*

Analysis

1. **Identify** what happened to the pH of the milk as time passed.

_____

_____

_____

_____

2. **Infer** what the change in pH means about the populations of microorganisms in the milk.

_____

_____

_____

_____

3. **Critical Thinking**
   Evaluating Results How does this model confirm the model of succession in Glacier Bay?

_____

_____

_____

_____

_____

Copyright © by Holt, Rinehart and Winston. All rights reserved.

Data Lab

Predicting How Predation Would Affect a Plant Species

Background

Grazing is the predation of plants by animals. Some plant species, such as *Gilia*, respond to grazing by growing new stems. Consider a field in which a large number of these plants are growing and being eaten by herbivores.

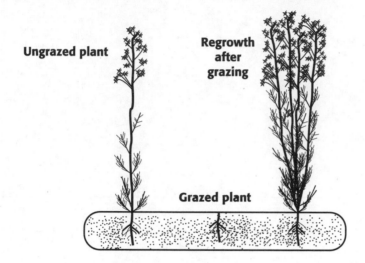

Analysis

1. Identify the plant that is likely to produce more seeds.

_____

_____

_____

2. Explain how grazing affects this plant species.

_____

_____

_____

3. Evaluate the significance to its environment of the plant's regrowth pattern.

_____

_____

_____

Copyright © by Holt, Rinehart and Winston. All rights reserved.

Predicting How Predation Would Affect a Plant Species *continued*

4. Hypothesize how this plant species might be affected if individual plants did not produce new stems in response to grazing.

_____

_____

_____

_____

Copyright © by Holt, Rinehart and Winston. All rights reserved.

Name _____ Class _____ Date _____

Data Lab
Predicting Changes in a Realized Niche

Background

Two features of a niche that can be readily measured are the location where the species feeds and the size of its preferred prey. The darkest shade in the center of the graph indicates the prey size and feeding location most frequently selected by one bird species (called Species A).

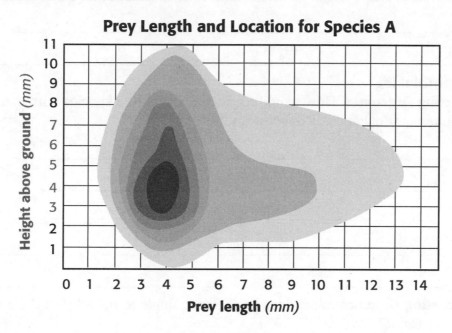

Prey Length and Location for Species A

Height above ground (mm) vs *Prey length (mm)*

Analysis

1. State the range of lengths of Species A's preferred prey.

_____

2. Identify the maximum height at which Species A feeds.

_____

3. Critical Thinking
   Predicting Outcomes Species B is introduced into Species A's feeding range. Species B has exactly the same feeding preferences, but it hunts at a slightly different time of day. How might this affect Species A?

_____

_____

_____

_____

Copyright © by Holt, Rinehart and Winston. All rights reserved.

Predicting Changes in a Realized Niche *continued*

4. Interpreting Graphics Species C is now introduced into Species A's feeding range. Species C feeds at the same time of day as Species A, but it prefers prey that are between 10 and 13 mm long. How might this affect Species A?

_____

_____

_____

_____

5. Critical Thinking
Predicting Outcomes How would the introduction of a species with exactly the same feeding habits as Species A affect the graph?

_____

_____

_____

_____

6. Interpreting Graphics What does the lightest shade at the edge of the contour lines represent?

_____

_____

Copyright © by Holt, Rinehart and Winston. All rights reserved.

Quick Lab)

Investigating Factors That Influence the Cooling of Earth's Surface

You can discover how the amount of water in an environment affects the rate at which that environment cools.

MATERIALS

- MBL or CBL system with appropriate software
- temperature probes
- test tubes
- beaker
- hot plate
- one-holed stoppers
- water
- sand
- test-tube tongs
- test-tube rack

Procedure

1. Set up an MBL/CBL system to collect and graph data from each temperature probe at 5-second intervals for 240 data points. Calibrate the probe using stored data.

2. Fill one test tube with water. Fill another test tube halfway with sand.

3. Place a temperature probe in the sand, and suspend another temperature probe at the same depth in the water, using one-holed stoppers to hold each temperature probe in place.

4. Place both test tubes in a beaker of hot water. Heat them to a temperature of about 70°C. **Caution: Hot water can burn skin.**

5. Using test-tube tongs, remove the test tubes and place them in the test-tube rack. Record the drop in temperature for 20 minutes.

Analysis

1. **Critical Thinking**
   Analyzing Results Did the two test tubes cool at the same rate? Offer an explanation for your observations.

   _____

   _____

2. **Critical Thinking**
   Predicting Outcomes In which biome—tropical rain forest or desert—would you expect the air temperature to drop most rapidly? Explain your answer.

   _____

   _____

Copyright © by Holt, Rinehart and Winston. All rights reserved.

Name _____ Class _____ Date _____

Modeling the Greenhouse Effect

You can use a quart jar to explore the greenhouse effect.

MATERIALS

- MBL or CBL system with appropriate software
- 2 temperature probes
- 1 qt jar
- lid with a 0.5 cm hole in the center
- tape
- heat source

Procedure

1. Set up an MBL/CBL system to collect data from two temperature probes at 6 second intervals for 150 data points.

2. Insert the end of one probe into the hole in the lid of a quart jar, and tape the probe in place. Place the other probe about 4 in. from the jar and at the same height as the first probe.

3. Place the jar about 30 cm from a heat-radiating source, and begin collecting data.

4. After 5 minutes, turn off (or remove) the heat source. Collect data for another 10 minutes.

Analysis

1. **Propose** an explanation for any differences between the two probes.

_____

_____

_____

_____

2. **Critical Thinking**
   Comparing Functions How does carbon dioxide gas in the atmosphere function in a way similar to the glass jar?

_____

_____

_____

Copyright © by Holt, Rinehart and Winston. All rights reserved.

Modeling the Greenhouse Effect *continued*

3. Critical Thinking
Predicting Outcomes How would the temperature on Earth be different if there were no carbon dioxide in the atmosphere?

_____

_____

_____

Copyright © by Holt, Rinehart and Winston. All rights reserved.

Quick Lab)   **DATASHEET FOR IN-TEXT LAB**

Modeling True Multicellularity

In order to understand the advantage that true multicellular organisms have over colonial organisms, you will model multicellular and colonial life.

MATERIALS

- two 15 ft lengths of rope
- several objects in the classroom

Procedure

1. Working as a class, divide into two groups. One group will model a colonial organism, and the other will model a true multicellular organism. Your teacher will loosely tie a rope around each group.

2. One student in each group will receive a set of instructions for collecting objects from around the classroom.

3. As each group carries out its instructions, students modeling the true multicellular organism may talk with one another, but students modeling the colonial organism must remain silent.

Analysis

1. **Identify** which group finished the assigned task first.

_____

2. **Infer** why the first group to finish was able to accomplish its task so quickly.

_____

3. **Choose** which type of organism is more advanced. Explain.

_____

_____

4. **Predict** how the more advanced organism could become more efficient.

_____

_____

_____

Copyright © by Holt, Rinehart and Winston. All rights reserved.

Quick Lab)

Observing Characteristics of Diatoms

Try this activity to find out why diatomaceous earth is used to make abrasives, fine filters, and reflective paints.

MATERIALS

- pipet
- water
- microscope slide
- toothpick
- diatomaceous earth
- coverslip
- compound microscope

Procedure

1. Using a pipet, place a drop of water in the center of a clean microscope slide.
2. Use a toothpick to scoop up a small amount of diatomaceous earth and mix it with the water drop. Add a coverslip.
3. Observe your wet mount under both low and high power of a compound microscope.
4. Draw some of the diatoms you see.
5. Observe the wetmount under low power as your partner shines a flashlight (at a 45° angle) on the slide. Turn off the microscope's light source so that only the flashlight is lighting the slide. Record your observations.

Analysis

1. **Label** your drawings as radial or bilateral. Find out the meanings of these terms and how they apply to your diatom drawings.

_____

_____

_____

_____

2. **Select** some characteristics you observed that are useful in classifying particular species of diatoms.

_____

3. **Interpret** what you observed when the flashlight was shone on the slide.

_____

_____

Copyright © by Holt, Rinehart and Winston. All rights reserved.

Name _____ Class _____ Date _____

Interpreting Competition Among Protists

Background

Protists, like all organisms, must compete with one another for nutrients. To examine the effects of competition between two species of *Paramecium*, equal numbers of the paramecia were grown together (dashed lines) and separately (solid lines). Study the graph at right, and answer the following questions.

Competition in Paramecia

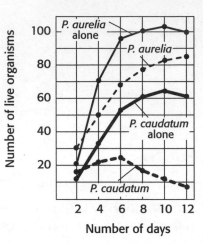

Analysis

1. Identify the *Paramecium* that grew best alone.

_____

2. Identify the variables in this experiment.

_____

_____

_____

3. Critical Thinking
Analyzing Data How would you explain the difference in the growth curves in the group that had both organisms?

_____

_____

4. Critical Thinking
Predicting Outcomes In a natural setting there would be more than two organisms present. Predict the effect that the presence of other organisms would have on the growth of the two species of *Paramecium*.

_____

_____

_____

Copyright © by Holt, Rinehart and Winston. All rights reserved.

Name _____ Class _____ Date _____

DATASHEET FOR IN-TEXT LAB

Observing Bread Mold

You can use a microscope to see the individual threads of cells that make up the body of a fungus.

MATERIALS

• prepared slide of *Rhizopus*—black bread mold

• compound microscope

Procedure

1. Examine a slide of black bread mold under low power of a microscope.

2. Move the slide to an area where you can clearly see threadlike structures.

3. Draw what you see in your lab notebook. Be sure to use at least one-third of the page.

4. Move the slide to examine an area where you can clearly see the round bulb-like structures.

5. Draw what you see in your notebook.

Analysis

1. Label the drawings you made, including the hyphae and mycelium.

_____

2. Explain where you would find each structure on a loaf of bread.

_____

_____

3. Critical Thinking
Recognizing Relationships Relate the structures you drew to their functions described in your textbook.

_____

_____

_____

Copyright © by Holt, Rinehart and Winston. All rights reserved.

Name _____ Class _____ Date _____

Data Lab

Analyzing the Effect of Mycorrhizae

Background

Two groups of plants were planted in similar soils under similar conditions, but group A was grown in sterilized soil and group B was grown in nonsterilized soil. After 18 weeks of growth, a photograph was taken of the plants. Examine the drawing, and answer the following questions:

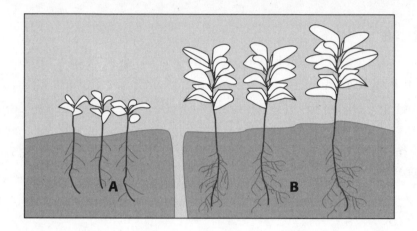

Analysis

1. Compare the growth of the two groups. Which grew faster?

_____

2. Explain why one group grew better than the other group.

_____

_____

3. Critical Thinking
Inferring Relationships Suggest a possible cause of slower growth in the smaller plants.

_____

_____

4. Recommend a course of action to restore growth in the stunted plants.

_____

Copyright © by Holt, Rinehart and Winston. All rights reserved.

Quick Lab

Observing the Behavior of Stomata

You can use nail polish to see that a leaf has many stomata.

MATERIALS

- clear nail polish
- plant kept in light
- plant kept in darkness
- two 4–5 cm strips of clear tape
- 2 microscope slides
- compound microscope

Procedure

1. Paint a thin layer of clear nail polish on a 1 × 1 cm area of a leaf on a plant kept in light. Do the same using a plant kept in darkness. Let the nail polish dry for 5 minutes.

2. Place a 4–5 cm strip of clear tape over the nail polish on each leaf. Press the tape firmly to the nail polish.

3. Carefully pull the tape off each leaf. Stick each piece of tape to a microscope slide. Label it appropriately.

4. View each slide with a microscope, first under low power and then under high power.

5. Draw and label what you see on each slide.

Analysis

1. **Describe** any differences in the stomata of the two plants.

_____

_____

_____

2. **Critical Thinking**
   Drawing Conclusions Which plant will lose water more quickly? Explain.

_____

_____

_____

_____

Copyright © by Holt, Rinehart and Winston. All rights reserved.

| Data Lab | DATASHEET FOR IN-TEXT LAB |

Analyzing the Effect of Climate on Plants

Background

The map below shows the taiga of North America. The taiga is a vast forest of conifers, a type of gymnosperm. The graph shows average annual temperature and precipitation data for Anchorage, Alaska, which is located at the western edge of the taiga. Use the map and graph to answer the questions on the next page.

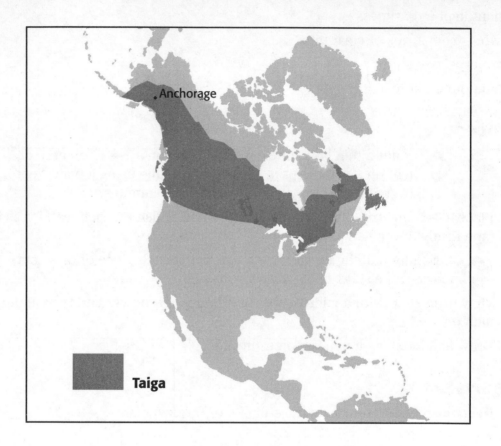

Taiga

Anchorage, Alaska

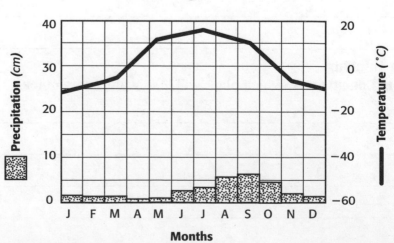

Copyright © by Holt, Rinehart and Winston. All rights reserved.

Analyzing the Effect of Climate on Plants *continued*

Analysis

1. **Describe** the climate of Anchorage, Alaska.

_____

_____

_____

_____

2. **Critical Thinking**
   Predicting Patterns What type of climate would you expect to find in other parts of the taiga?

_____

_____

_____

3. **Critical Thinking**
   Drawing Conclusions Does climate appear to be an important factor in where the conifers of the taiga grow? Explain.

_____

_____

_____

_____

Copyright © by Holt, Rinehart and Winston. All rights reserved.

Distinguishing Fruits and Vegetables

You can find out if a plant product is a fruit by cutting it open and examining its internal structure.

MATERIALS

- apple
- banana
- green bean
- potato
- squash
- tomato
- plastic knife

Procedure

1. Look at several familiar fruits and vegetables. Classify each one as either a fruit or a vegetable in the familiar sense.

2. ◆ **CAUTION: Sharp objects can cause injury. Handle knives carefully.** Use a plastic knife to cut open each fruit and vegetable.

3. Look at the fruits and vegetables again. Classify each by its botanical function—either a fruit or a vegetative part.

Analysis

1. **Compare** the familiar and botanical classifications you gave each fruit and vegetable.

_____

_____

_____

_____

2. **Critical Thinking**
   Analyzing Data Which fruits and vegetables did you classify differently?

_____

_____

_____

Copyright © by Holt, Rinehart and Winston. All rights reserved.

Distinguishing Fruits and Vegetables *continued*

3. Critical Thinking
Analyzing Results Defend the classifications you made for item 2.

_____

_____

_____

_____

_____

4. Critical Thinking
Drawing Conclusions Based on your data, when is a vegetable a fruit?

_____

_____

Copyright © by Holt, Rinehart and Winston. All rights reserved.

Name _____ Class _____ Date _____

Observing a Fern Gametophyte

You can observe the archegonia and antheridia of a fern gametophyte with a microscope.

MATERIALS

• prepared slide of a fern gametophyte with archegonia and antheridia

• compound microscope

Procedure

1. Examine a slide of a fern gametophyte under low power of a microscope. Move the slide until you can see a cluster of archegonia. Now, switch to high power, and focus on one archegonium. Draw and label what you see. Use a separate sheet of paper.

2. Switch back to low power, and move the slide until you can see several egg-shaped structures. These are antheridia. Now, switch to high power, and focus on one antheridium. Draw and label what you see.

Analysis

1. **Describe** the appearance of an archegonium and an antheridium.

_____

_____

_____

_____

2. **Critical Thinking**
Drawing Conclusions In which structure, an archegonium or antheridium, does the growth of a new sporophyte begin? Explain.

_____

_____

_____

_____

_____

Copyright © by Holt, Rinehart and Winston. All rights reserved.

Quick Lab   **DATASHEET FOR IN-TEXT LAB**

Observing the Gametophytes of Pines

You can observe the gametophytes of a pine with a microscope.

MATERIALS

• prepared slides of the following: male pine cone, female pine cone, pine ovule

• hand lens

• compound microscope

Procedure

1. Examine prepared slides of male and female pine cones first with a hand lens and then under the low power of a microscope.

2. Make a sketch of each type of pine cone, and label the structures that you recognize.

3. Examine a prepared slide of a pine ovule under the low power of a compound microscope. Compare what you see with the drawing.

4. Draw a pine ovule, and label the following structures: scale, ovule, egg, pollen tube (if visible).

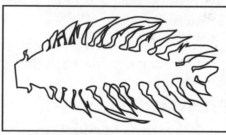

Immature female pine cone

Analysis

1. **Compare** and **Contrast** the structure and contents of male and female pine cones.

   _____

   _____

   _____

   _____

2. **Critical Thinking**

   Applying Information It takes 15 months for a pine pollen tube to grow through the wall of a pine ovule. How would you describe the rate of pollen-tube growth in pines?

   _____

   _____

Copyright © by Holt, Rinehart and Winston. All rights reserved.

DATASHEET FOR IN-TEXT LAB

Observing the Arrangement of Parts of a Flower

You can see how the parts of flowers are arranged by dissecting flowers.

MATERIALS

- gloves
- monocot flower
- dicot flower
- paper
- tape

Procedure

1. Put on gloves. Examine a monocot flower and a dicot flower. Locate the sepals, petals, stamens, and pistil of each flower.

2. Separate the parts of each flower, and tape them to a piece of paper. Label each set of parts.

3. Count the number of petals, sepals, and stamens in each flower. Record this information below each flower.

Analysis

1. **Compare** and **Contrast** the appearance of the sepals and petals of each flower.

   _____

   _____

2. **Critical Thinking**
   Forming a Hypothesis For each flower, suggest a function for the petals based on their appearance.

   _____

   _____

   _____

3. **Critical Thinking**
   Justifying Conclusions Explain why each flower is from either a monocot or a dicot.

   _____

   _____

   _____

Copyright © by Holt, Rinehart and Winston. All rights reserved.

Name _____ Class _____ Date _____

Comparing the Structures of Roots and Stems

You can use a microscope to see differences in the internal structure of roots and stems.

MATERIALS

- compound microscope
- prepared slide of a cross section of the following: dicot root, monocot root, dicot stem, monocot stem

Procedure

1. View cross sections of dicot and monocot roots with a compound microscope. For each, draw and label what you see under low power. Then look at the vascular tissue in each root under high power. Draw what you see in each root, and label the xylem and phloem.

2. View cross sections of dicot and monocot stems with a compound microscope. For each, draw and label what you see under low power. Then look at a vascular bundle in each stem under high power. Draw each vascular bundle, and label the xylem and phloem.

Analysis

1. **Compare and contrast** the location of xylem and phloem in roots and stems.

_____

_____

_____

_____

2. **Compare and contrast** the arrangement and structure of the vascular bundles in monocot and dicot stems.

_____

_____

_____

_____

_____

Copyright © by Holt, Rinehart and Winston. All rights reserved.

Comparing the Structures of Roots and Stems *continued*

3. Describe the relationship between the structure and function of vascular tissue.

_____

_____

_____

_____

_____

Copyright © by Holt, Rinehart and Winston. All rights reserved.

Quick Lab

Observing the Structures Inside a Leaf

With a microscope, you can see how a leaf is put together.

MATERIALS

- prepared slide of a leaf cross section
- compound microscope

Procedure

1. View a cross section of a leaf under low power of a compound microscope. Then switch to high power.

2. Identify the following structures: stoma, guard cells, upper and lower epidermis, palisade layer, spongy layer, and vein.

Analysis

1. **Describe** a stoma, and relate the function of a stoma to your description.

_____

_____

_____

2. **Describe** the location and contents of the veins.

_____

_____

_____

3. **Critical Thinking**
   Relating Concepts How do the location and structure of the palisade and spongy layers help a leaf perform photosynthesis?

_____

_____

_____

_____

_____

Copyright © by Holt, Rinehart and Winston. All rights reserved.

Name _____ Class _____ Date _____

Inferring the Rate of Transpiration

Background

The graph shows the rate of water movement in a plant during high humidity and during low humidity. The rate of water movement indicates the rate of transpiration. Use the graph to answer the questions below.

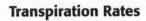

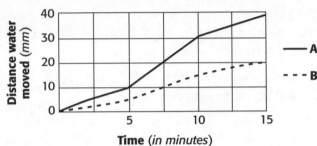

Analysis

1. Determine how far water had moved after 10 minutes under the condition represented by curve A.

_____

2. Critical Thinking
Analyzing Results After 15 minutes, how much farther had water moved under condition A than under condition B?

_____

3. Critical Thinking
Recognizing Relationships Which curve indicates a lower transpiration rate? Explain your reasoning.

_____

_____

_____

4. Critical Thinking
Drawing Conclusions Which curve shows the transpiration rate during low humidity? Justify your answer.

_____

_____

_____

Copyright © by Holt, Rinehart and Winston. All rights reserved.

Name _____ Class _____ Date _____

Investigating the Effects of Ethylene on a Plant

You can use a ripe apple to see one of the effects of ethylene on plants.

MATERIALS
- 4 L glass jars with lids (2)
- 2 plants in 5 cm pots
- small ripe apple

Procedure
1. Place a plant inside one of the jars. Tightly secure the lid.

2. Place the other plant and the apple inside the other jar. Tightly secure the lid.

3. Observe both jars for several days. Record what you see.

Analysis
1. Describe any changes in the plant in each jar.

_____

_____

_____

2. Critical Thinking
Drawing Conclusions A ripe apple gives off ethylene gas. Based on your observations, how does ethylene affect a plant?

_____

_____

_____

Copyright © by Holt, Rinehart and Winston. All rights reserved.

Name _____ Class _____ Date _____

Data Lab

Interpreting Annual Rings

Background

The annual rings of a woody stem provide important clues to annual variations in the rainfall an area receives over time. Thick rings form in years with heavy rainfall. Relatively thin rings form in dry years. Use the picture to answer the questions that follow.

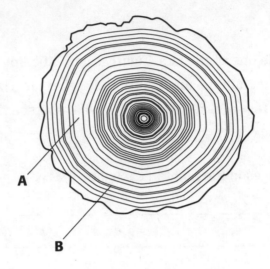

Analysis

1. **Critical Thinking**
   Interpreting Data What do the annual rings indicate about the climate where this plant grew?

   _____

   _____

2. **Critical Thinking**
   Drawing Conclusions Which ring, A or B, indicates a year when this plant received more rainfall?

   _____

3. **Critical Thinking**
   Making Predictions How will the annual rings of a nearby tree of the same age and species compare with those of this tree?

   _____

   _____

Copyright © by Holt, Rinehart and Winston. All rights reserved.

Name _____ Class _____ Date _____

Analyzing the Effect of Cold on Seed Germination

Background

In some plants, a period of low temperatures is needed to break seed dormancy. The graph shows how being stored at a low temperature (4°C) affected the ability of apple seeds to germinate. Use the graph to answer the questions that follow.

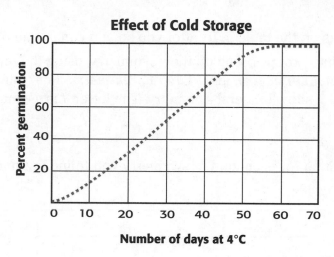

Effect of Cold Storage

Analysis

1. **Summarize** the overall effect of cold temperatures on the germination of apple seeds.

_____

2. **Calculate** the number of weeks that apple seeds must be stored at 4°C for at least 80 percent of the seeds to germinate.

_____

3. **Critical Thinking**
   Interpreting Graphs What percentage of apple seeds germinate after storage at 4°C for 20 days?

_____

4. **Critical Thinking**
   Predicting Patterns What percentage of apple seeds will germinate after being stored at 4°C for 80 days?

_____

Copyright © by Holt, Rinehart and Winston. All rights reserved.

Quick Lab   **DATASHEET FOR IN-TEXT LAB**

Recognizing Symmetry

You can use the letters of the alphabet to better understand the
nature of symmetry.

MATERIALS

• envelope containing letters of the alphabet

Procedure

1. Spread the letters on the table in front of you so you can see all of them.

2. Sort the letters into groups based on their symmetry, using the terms
   asymmetry, *radial symmetry*, and *bilateral symmetry*. For example,
   the letters *A* and *T* show bilateral symmetry. The letter *J* is asymmetrical.

Analysis

1. **Propose** a definition for each kind of symmetry you found in the letters.

   _____

   _____

   _____

   _____

   _____

   _____

2. **List** any letters you found difficult to classify, explaining why it was difficult
   to classify these letters.

   _____

   _____

   _____

   _____

3. **Identify** the letters that show the same kind of symmetry as sponges.

   _____

4. **Identify** two or three animals that you might be familiar with that have the
   same kind of symmetry as the letter *M*.

   _____

Copyright © by Holt, Rinehart and Winston. All rights reserved.

Recognizing Symmetry *continued*

5. Critical Thinking

Evaluating Methods What are some strengths and weaknesses of using symmetry as a way of classifying or describing organisms?

_____

_____

_____

_____

_____

Copyright © by Holt, Rinehart and Winston. All rights reserved.

Data Lab

Exploring the Animal Kingdom

Background

You can find out more about the animal phyla by referring to the section "A Six-Kingdom System" in the Appendix. Turn to this section and locate the information for kingdom Animalia. Follow the procedure below to evaluate this information.

Procedure

1. Read the introductory paragraph for kingdom Animalia. Then quickly skim over the information presented. Do not read it word for word, but observe how the information is divided into sections.

2. Choose one phylum, and read all of the information about it.

3. As you read, notice how color is used and what types of information are given, for example, number of species found and habitat.

Analysis

1. List at least three types of information you found for the phylum you read about.

_____

_____

_____

2. Analyze how color is used to distinguish between the different entries on a page.

_____

_____

_____

3. Propose a way that you might use this information when studying about a particular animal phylum.

_____

_____

_____

_____

Copyright © by Holt, Rinehart and Winston. All rights reserved.

Math Lab)   **DATASHEET FOR IN-TEXT LAB**

Calculating Filtration Rate in the Human Kidney

Background

The human kidney filters fluid from the blood at the rate of approximately 125 mL per minute. However, only a small percentage of this fluid is excreted as urine—adult humans normally excrete between 1.5 and 2.3 L of urine a day.

Analysis

1. **Calculate** how many milliliters of fluid the human kidneys filter each hour.

   _____

2. **Calculate** how many milliliters of fluid the kidneys filter each day.

   _____

3. **Critical Thinking**
   Analyzing Data Convert your answer in item 2 from milliliters to liters. For help, see "Math and Problem-Solving Skills: SI Measurement" in the Appendix. To better visualize the quantity of fluid represented by your answer, think about the volume of fluid contained in a 1 L bottle of soda.

   _____

4. **Critical Thinking**
   Predicting Outcomes What would happen if the kidneys could not return water to the body?

   _____

   _____

Copyright © by Holt, Rinehart and Winston. All rights reserved.

Name _____ Class _____ Date _____

Estimating Size Using a Microscope

You can use the microscope to estimate the size of cnidarians that are too small to measure directly.

MATERIALS

• transparent millimeter ruler

• compound microscope with low-power objective or a dissecting microscope

• prepared slide of a medusa or polyp

Procedure

1. Identify the millimeter marks along the edge of the ruler.

2. With the microscope on low power (4× or lower), place the ruler on the stage and focus on the millimeter marks.

3. Adjust the ruler so that one edge lies across the diameter of the field, as shown. Then measure the diameter of the field of view in millimeters.

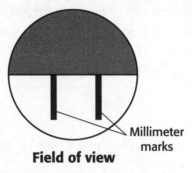

Millimeter
marks

Field of view

4. Remove the ruler, and place the prepared slide on the stage. Identify the tentacles, gastrovascular cavity, and mouth.

5. Estimate the length and width of your organism as a ratio of the width of the field of view. For example, the length of your organism may appear to cover about two-thirds of the field of view.

Analysis

1. Calculate the size of your organism in millimeters by multiplying the ratio you found in step 5 by the width of the field of view you found in step 3.

_____

_____

2. Describe the body plan of the organism you viewed using terms from step 4.

_____

_____

Copyright © by Holt, Rinehart and Winston. All rights reserved.

Name _____ Class _____ Date _____

Quick Lab
Observing Planarian Behavior

Most bilaterally symmetrical organisms have sense organs concentrated in one end of the animal. You can observe how this arrangement affects the way they explore their environment.

MATERIALS
- eyedropper
- live culture of planaria
- small culture dish with pond water
- hand lens or dissecting microscope
- forceps
- small piece of raw liver (3–7 cm)

Procedure
1. Using the tip of the eyedropper, place a planarian in the culture dish with pond water.
2. Using the hand lens or dissecting microscope, observe the planarian as it adjusts to its environment. Determine which end of the planarian contains sensory apparatus for exploring the environment.
3. Using forceps, place the liver in the pond water about 1 cm behind the planarian.
4. Observe the planarian's response. If the planarian approaches the liver, move the liver to a different position.
5. Continue observing the planarian for 5 minutes, moving the liver frequently.

Analysis
1. **Describe** the planarian's means of locomotion.

_____

_____

_____

2. **Describe** how the planarian responded to the liver.

_____

_____

_____

Copyright © by Holt, Rinehart and Winston. All rights reserved.

Observing Planarian Behavior *continued*

3. Contrast the feeding behavior of planarians with that of hydras.

_____

_____

_____

_____

_____

_____

4. Critical Thinking

Evaluating an Argument Evaluate this statement: Bilateral symmetry gives planaria an advantage when feeding because sensory organs are concentrated in one end. Support your opinion with the observations you made on planaria.

_____

_____

_____

_____

Copyright © by Holt, Rinehart and Winston. All rights reserved.

Identifying Parasites

Background

This graph shows how two drugs affect the release of eggs in a human infested with two parasites—*Schistosoma* and *Ascaris*. Drug 1 works by killing adult parasites in the intestines. Drug 2 works by killing adult parasites in the blood vessels. Use the graph and your knowledge of parasitic infections to answer the analysis questions.

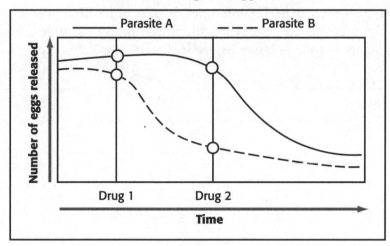

Effects of Drugs on Egg Release

Analysis

1. Describe the response of the parasites to the two different drug treatments.

_____

_____

2. Identify the main human organs and tissues infected by the adult stages of *Schistosoma* and *Ascaris*.

_____

3. Identify which curve on the graph shows *Schistosoma* egg production and which shows *Ascaris* egg production.

_____

Copyright © by Holt, Rinehart and Winston. All rights reserved.

4. Critical Thinking
Justifying Conclusions Explain why you made the identifications you did in item 3.

_____

_____

_____

_____

5. Critical Thinking
Forming Hypotheses *Schistosoma* spends part of its life cycle as a parasite of snails. Hypothesize a reason for an increase in the number of cases of schistosomiasis in villages near where hydroelectric dams have been built.

_____

_____

_____

Copyright © by Holt, Rinehart and Winston. All rights reserved.

Modeling an Open Circulatory System

You can model an open circulatory system using simple items to represent the heart, blood vessels, blood, and body tissues of a living organism.

MATERIALS

- surgical tubing, 15 cm (about 6 in.) piece
- clear plastic tubing, 15 cm (about 6 in.) and 7.5 cm (about 3 in.) pieces
- shallow pan filled with water
- eyedropper
- food coloring

PROCEDURE

1. Connect the surgical tubing to the two pieces of clear plastic tubing.
2. Place the tubing into the tray filled with water. Allow the tubing to fill with water and rest on the bottom.
3. With the tubing still submerged, use an eyedropper to place two drops of food coloring into the short piece of clear plastic tubing.
4. With your thumb and index finger, squeeze along the piece of surgical tubing to pump the food coloring through the system.
5. As you continue to pump, observe the movement of food coloring.

Analysis

1. Describe what happened when you squeezed along the tubing.

   _____

   _____

   _____

2. Identify the structures represented by the pan of water, the surgical tubing, and the clear plastic tubing.

   _____

   _____

   _____

   _____

   _____

Copyright © by Holt, Rinehart and Winston. All rights reserved.

Modeling an Open Circulatory System *continued*

3. Critical Thinking
Evaluating Results Evaluate your model's efficiency at pumping blood through the system.

_____

_____

_____

_____

4. Critical Thinking
Analyzing Methods How does this model differ from a real circulatory system?

_____

_____

_____

5. Critical Thinking
Analyzing Methods How could you modify the model to make it more accurate?

_____

_____

Copyright © by Holt, Rinehart and Winston. All rights reserved.

DATASHEET FOR IN-TEXT LAB
Analyzing the Molluscan Body Plan

Background
Mollusks share many common characteristics, yet there is great variety among the classes. The drawings below show how the shell and foot vary in three classes of mollusks. Use the drawings to answer the analysis questions.

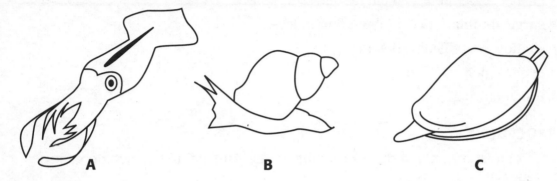

A   **B**   **C**

Analysis
1. Determine the class of mollusk *A*, mollusk *B*, and mollusk *C*.

_____

2. Compare the shell modifications. Why might a shell suited to one mollusk be inappropriate for another?

_____

_____

3. Critical Thinking
Identifying Functions For each class shown, explain how the foot is useful for the animal's environment or kind of movement.

_____

_____

_____

4. Critical Thinking
Predicting Outcomes Terrestrial snails and slugs are nearly identical except that slugs do not have a shell. Acidic forest soils are often poor in minerals, including calcium. Alkaline or neutral soils are rich in minerals. In which kind of soil would you be more likely to find a slug? Explain your answer.

_____

_____

Copyright © by Holt, Rinehart and Winston. All rights reserved.

Quick Lab

Modeling a Closed Circulatory System

You can model a closed circulatory system using simple items to represent the heart, blood vessels, blood, and body tissues of a living organism.

MATERIALS

- clear plastic tubing, 30 cm (about 12 in.) piece
- surgical tubing, 15 cm (about 6 in.) piece
- shallow pan filled with water
- eyedropper
- food coloring

PROCEDURE

1. Connect one end of the clear tubing to the surgical tubing. Submerge in the pan.

2. Use the eyedropper to insert several drops of food coloring into the surgical tubing. Close the tubing by attaching the two free ends together.

3. With your thumb and index finger, squeeze along the piece of surgical tubing to pump the food coloring through the system.

4. Observe the food coloring as it moves through the tubing.

Analysis

1. Describe what happened when you pumped the food coloring through the system.

_____

_____

2. Identify what structures the pan of water, the surgical tubing, and the clear plastic tubing represent.

_____

_____

_____

3. Evaluate your model's efficiency at pumping blood through the system.

_____

_____

Copyright © by Holt, Rinehart and Winston. All rights reserved.

Modeling a Closed Circulatory System *continued*

4. Critical Thinking

Analyzing Methods How could you modify the model to make it more accurate?

_____

_____

_____

_____

5. Critical Thinking

Inferring Relationships If you did the Quick Lab in the previous section that models an open circulatory system, recall what happened in that system. Which model do you think exerted a greater pressure on the fluid in the tube?

_____

_____

Copyright © by Holt, Rinehart and Winston. All rights reserved.

Quick Lab

Evaluating Jointed Appendages

To understand the importance of jointed appendages, test your range of movement without and with bending your joints.

MATERIALS

- meterstick
- paper
- pencil

Procedure

1. Work in pairs, and assign one person to be the test subject and one person to record the data.

2. The test subject extends one arm straight out in front of the body. The subject then places a meterstick along the inside of the arm. The elbow should not be bent.

3. The recorder measures and records the distance along the meterstick that the test subject can reach with extended (not bent) fingers.

4. The test subject now tries to increase the range of movement by bending the fingers only. The recorder measures and records the closest and farthest distance along the meterstick that can be reached.

5. The test subject now tries to increase the range of motion by bending the elbow. The recorder measures and records the closest and farthest distance along the meterstick that can be reached.

Analysis

1. **Describe** how eating breakfast might be different if you did not have joints on your fingers and at your elbows.

_____

2. **Predict** the advantages an animal with jointed appendages has over an animal without jointed appendages when capturing and consuming food.

_____

_____

3. **Predict** the advantages for an arthropod that has sense organs (eyes and odor detectors) on the ends of jointed appendages.

_____

_____

_____

Copyright © by Holt, Rinehart and Winston. All rights reserved.

Data Lab

Analyzing the Effects of Pesticide Use

Background

In nature, insect pests are usually kept in balance by the presence of predators, including other insects. The use of some pesticides can upset this balance, as shown in the graph below. Examine the graph, and answer the analysis questions.

Changes in Two Insect Populations

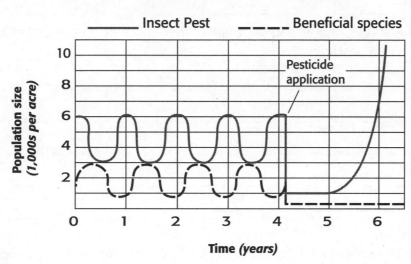

Analysis

1. Identify the years during which the two insect populations appear to maintain stability in relation to each other. Justify your answer with data from the graph.

_____

_____

_____

_____

2. Describe the relationship between the two insect species before year 4.

_____

_____

_____

_____

_____

Copyright © by Holt, Rinehart and Winston. All rights reserved.

Analyzing the Effects of Pesticide Use *continued*

3. Describe the changes in the two populations after the use of a pesticide.

_____

_____

_____

_____

_____

4. Compare the annual changes in population size of the pest species before and after the use of a pesticide.

_____

_____

_____

_____

_____

5. Critical Thinking
Developing Hypotheses Propose a hypothesis that might explain the dramatic changes that occur in the insect populations after the use of pesticides.

_____

_____

_____

_____

_____

Copyright © by Holt, Rinehart and Winston. All rights reserved.

Name _____ Class _____ Date _____

Relating Molting to Mortality Rates

Background

During the soft-shell stage that follows molting, many crustaceans die of disease or are eaten by predators. The bar graph below shows the percent mortality for crabs over a 9-month period. Study the data, and answer the analysis questions.

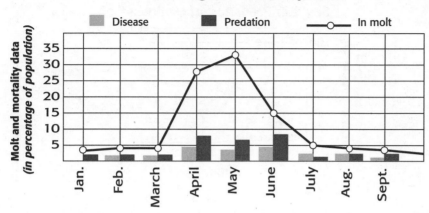

Molting and Mortality Rates

Analysis

1. **Summarize** what the data in the graph tell you about crab mortality.

   _____

2. **Summarize** what the graph shows about molting in crabs.

   _____

3. **Describe** the relationship between the mortality rates and molting periods of crabs.

   _____

4. **Critical Thinking**
   Developing Hypotheses Propose a hypothesis that explains the relationship between the percent of crabs molting and mortality rates.

   _____

5. **Critical Thinking**
   Making Predictions Most states have laws that require crab fishers to return molting crabs to the water. How might the length of time a molting crab is exposed to air or how roughly a crab is handled affect whether the crab survives being caught and released?

   _____

   _____

Copyright © by Holt, Rinehart and Winston. All rights reserved.

Name _____ Class _____ Date _____

Determining How Predators Affect Prey

Background

Sea stars can be very effective predators, and they frequently eat mollusks. The graph below shows the relative number of two species of mollusks before and after the introduction of a predatory sea star. Study the graph, and answer the Analysis questions.

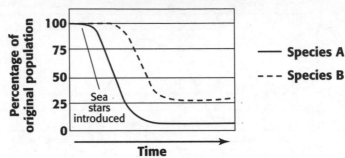

Sea Star Predation of Mollusks

Analysis

1. **Compare** the relative sizes of the two mollusk populations before the introduction of the sea star.

   _____

   _____

   _____

2. **Identify** the preferred prey of the sea star, and use the data presented in the graph to support your answer.

   _____

   _____

   _____

3. **Critical Thinking**
   Analyzing Data When the sea star began preying on the nonpreferred species, the preferred species had dropped to what percent of its original population?

   _____

   _____

Copyright © by Holt, Rinehart and Winston. All rights reserved.

Determining How Predators Affect Prey *continued*

4. Critical Thinking
Inferring Relationships What factors might cause the sea star to begin consuming a nonpreferred species, even when its preferred prey is still present?

_____

_____

_____

_____

_____

5. Critical Thinking
Predicting Outcomes Predict the relative abundance of the two species of mollusks if the sea star remains in the area indefinitely.

_____

_____

_____

_____

_____

_____

Copyright © by Holt, Rinehart and Winston. All rights reserved.

DATASHEET FOR IN-TEXT LAB

Comparing the Structures of the Notochord and Nerve Cord

The notochord and hollow nerve cord are two important characteristics of all chordates. While both are located on an animal's dorsal side, they differ in size, structure, and location. You can compare the two when viewing a cross section of an adult lancelet.

MATERIALS

• compound microscope

• prepared slide of the cross section of an adult lancelet

Procedure

1. Place a prepared slide of a cross section of an adult lancelet under the microscope.

2. Locate the dorsal side of the specimen, and turn the slide so the dorsal side is on top.

3. Locate the notochord and hollow nerve cord. If visible, locate the intestine.

4. Sketch the specimen, and label the dorsal and ventral sides, the notochord, the nerve cord, and the intestines. Use a separate sheet of paper.

Analysis

1. **Describe** the structure, location, and size of the nerve cord and the notochord.

_____

_____

2. **Identify** the kind of symmetry observed in the adult lancelet.

_____

3. **Compare** the lancelet's symmetry with the symmetry of adult echinoderms.

_____

4. **Critical Thinking**
   Forming Hypotheses In vertebrate chordates, the notochord becomes a backbone that encases the nerve cord. Why might this arrangement be an advantage to an animal?

_____

_____

Copyright © by Holt, Rinehart and Winston. All rights reserved.

98 Echinoderms and Invertebrate Chordates

Data Lab
Using Timelines and Phylogenetic Trees

Background

Use the timeline in the Holt Biology chapter titled "History of Life on Earth" and the phylogenetic tree below to answer the analysis questions. Tell which graphic you used to answer each question.

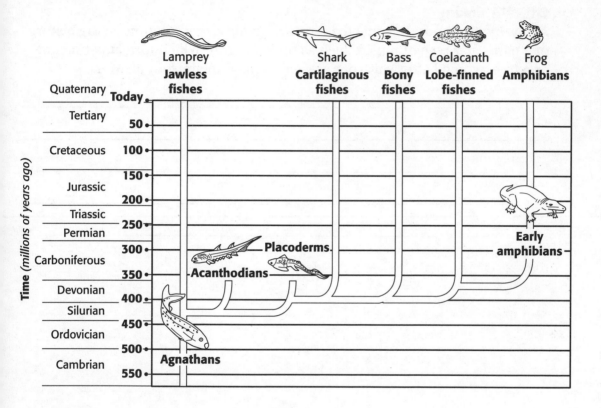

Analysis

1. Critical Thinking

Interpreting Graphics When the jawed fishes appeared, what was occurring on land?

_____

_____

2. Critical Thinking

Interpreting Graphics What are the approximate beginning and ending dates of the Ordovician period and the Silurian period?

_____

_____

Copyright © by Holt, Rinehart and Winston. All rights reserved.

| Using Timelines and Phylogenetic Trees *continued*

3. Critical Thinking

Interpreting Graphics Of the fishes living during the Devonian period, which groups have descendants living today?

_____

_____

_____

4. Critical Thinking

Analyzing Methods Imagine that you are giving a presentation on the history of a particular type of music, such as rock and roll. Which format, a timeline or a tree, would better suit your presentation? Explain your answer.

_____

_____

_____

_____

_____

Copyright © by Holt, Rinehart and Winston. All rights reserved.

Name _____ Class _____ Date _____

Comparing the Surface Areas of Gills

Background

Air contains more oxygen than water, so why do fish die when removed from water? To understand what happens to gills when they are removed from water, follow the procedure below.

MATERIALS

- cellophane wrap
- scissors
- toothpick
- ruler
- container of water

Procedure

1. Cut an 8 × 6 cm piece of cellophane wrap. Use the piece of wrap and a toothpick to make a model of fish gills, as shown in the drawing.

2. Measure the approximate length and width of the model. Calculate the area of the model by using the formula $a = l \times w$.

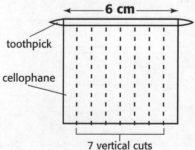

3. Submerge the model in water and allow it to float at the top. Notice any change in shape of the model.

4. Grasp the model by the toothpick and pull it gently through the water. Then remove the model and place it on the table.

5. Without rearranging the model in any way, measure its approximate length and width. Calculate the area of the model again.

Analysis

1. Summarize any difference you observed between the gill model in the water and the wet model out of the water.

_____

_____

2. Compare the area obtained in step 2 with that obtained in step 5. If the areas are different, identify which was larger.

_____

_____

Copyright © by Holt, Rinehart and Winston. All rights reserved.

Comparing the Surface Areas of Gills *continued*

3. Critical Thinking

Analyzing Data Consider what you know about the requirements for gas exchange across a gill's surface. Do the data you obtained suggest a reason why fishes cannot live out of water? Explain your answer.

_____

_____

_____

_____

4. Critical Thinking

Comparing Structures Your model is two-dimensional. To calculate the surface area of an actual gill, you would need to know another measurement. What is that measurement, and why is it important?

_____

_____

_____

_____

Copyright © by Holt, Rinehart and Winston. All rights reserved.

Name _____ Class _____ Date _____

DATASHEET FOR IN-TEXT LAB

Analyzing Ion Excretion in Fish

Background

A few species of fish, such as adult salmon, are able to move between salt-water and freshwater environments. The graph below shows the excreted ion concentration of a fish as it travels from one body of water to another. Examine the graph, and answer the analysis questions.

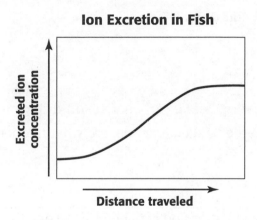

Analysis

1. Determine if the fish is losing or gaining ions by excretion as it travels.

_____

2. Critical Thinking
Inferring Conclusions Is the fish traveling from fresh water to salt water or from salt water to fresh water?

_____

3. Summarize the reasoning you used to answer item 2.

_____

_____

_____

_____

_____

_____

Copyright © by Holt, Rinehart and Winston. All rights reserved.

Modeling the Action of a Swim Bladder

Most fish use a swim bladder to regulate their depth in water. As gas enters the swim bladder, the fish rises in the water. As gas is expelled, the fish sinks to a lower depth.

MATERIALS

- 100 mL beaker or small glass
- cold, clear, carbonated soft drink
- 2 very dry raisins

Procedure

1. Fill a 100 mL beaker with a cold, carbonated soft drink.

2. Drop two raisins into the beaker, and observe what happens over the next 5 minutes.

Analysis

1. **Describe** what happened after you dropped the raisins into the soft drink.

_____

_____

_____

2. **Forming Hypotheses** Develop a hypothesis to explain your observations.

_____

_____

_____

_____

3. **Critical Thinking**
   Analyzing Results How does the lifting of the raisins differ from the use of a swim bladder to control buoyancy?

_____

_____

_____

_____

Copyright © by Holt, Rinehart and Winston. All rights reserved.

Modeling the Action of a Swim Bladder *continued*

4. Critical Thinking

Forming Reasoned Opinions Think about the energy you would have to expend to keep yourself in one position underwater. What advantage might a swim bladder provide to a fish?

_____

_____

_____

_____

_____

Copyright © by Holt, Rinehart and Winston. All rights reserved.

Data Lab

Identifying Ectotherms

Background

The body temperature of all animals changes during the course of a day. How it changes can help you identify an animal as an ectotherm or an endotherm.

Body Temperatures of Two Animals

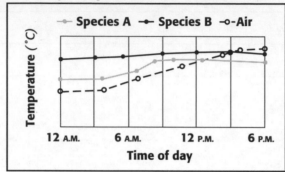

Analysis

1. **Analyze** the data and determine which animal species, A or B, is most likely an ectotherm. Explain your reasoning.

   _____

   _____

   _____

   _____

2. **Identify** the time of day the animal you identified as an ectotherm reaches its lowest body temperature.

   _____

3. **Identify** the time of day the animal you identified as an ectotherm reaches its highest body temperature.

   _____

4. **Propose** a reason why the ectotherm's body temperature is highest at this time.

   _____

5. **Predict** what the endotherm's graph line would look like if it were extended to show body temperature between 6 P.M. and midnight.

   _____

   _____

Copyright © by Holt, Rinehart and Winston. All rights reserved.

Quick Lab

Modeling Watertight Skin

Modeling Watertight Skin

Scales make a reptile's skin almost watertight. This is one of reptiles' adaptations to terrestrial life. You can use grapes to model and compare water loss in different types of skin.

MATERIALS

- forceps
- 2 grapes
- balance
- Petri dish

Procedure

1. Find the mass of one grape, and record it in the data table. Then place the grape in an open Petri dish.

2. Using forceps, peel the skin from the second grape. Find and record the mass of the peeled grape. Then place it in the same Petri dish, but do not let the two grapes touch.

3. Wait 15 minutes, and then find and record the mass of each grape again.

Data Table		
	Grape	**Peeled Grape**
Initial Mass		
Mass after 15 minutes		

Analysis

1. **Calculate** the difference between the original and final masses of each grape.

_____

_____

2. **Propose** an explanation for any changes in mass you observed.

_____

_____

_____

Copyright © by Holt, Rinehart and Winston. All rights reserved.

Modeling Watertight Skin *continued*

3. Determine which grape represents an amphibian's skin and which represents a reptile's skin.

_____

_____

4. Describe how a watertight skin is an adaptation to terrestrial life. Include information you have learned in this lab in your explanation.

_____

_____

_____

_____

Copyright © by Holt, Rinehart and Winston. All rights reserved.

Name _____ Class _____ Date _____

Math Lab

Calculating Average Bone Density

Background

Density is the ratio of the mass of an object to its volume. Several teams of students determined the density of bones from two different animals. You can use their data to practice calculating average bone density.

1. Add the densities of one bone type. For example, if three bone samples

Data Table				
Bone type	**Team 1**	**Team 2**	**Team 3**	**Team 4**
Animal 1	1.6 g/cm³	1.0 g/cm³	1.2 g/cm³	1.4 g/cm³
Animal 2	2.3 g/cm³	1.8 g/cm³	1.8 g/cm³	2.1 g/cm³

have densities of 3.0, 3.1, and 2.9 g/cm³, their sum would be 9.0 g/cm³.

2. Divide the sum of the densities by the number of samples.

$$\text{Average density} = \frac{\text{sum of the densities}}{\text{number of samples}} = \frac{9.0\text{g/cm}^3}{3} = 3.0\text{g/cm}^3$$

Analysis

1. Calculate the average bone density for each of the two animals in the data table. Express your answer in grams per cubic centimeter.

_____

2. Critical Thinking
Evaluating Methods Why is it important to analyze several samples and obtain the average of your data?

_____

_____

3. Critical Thinking
Drawing Conclusions Based on your answer to item 1, which of the two animals is more likely to be a bird?

_____

_____

Copyright © by Holt, Rinehart and Winston. All rights reserved.

Quick Lab

Evaluating the Insulation Value of Hair

When you are getting dressed on a cold day, why are you are more likely to choose a wool sweater than a cotton one? In this lab, you will compare the insulating abilities of the animal fiber wool and the vegetable fiber cotton.

MATERIALS

- MBL or CBL system with appropriate software
- temperature probe
- 1 wool sock
- beaker of ice
- graph paper (optional)
- 1 cotton sock

Procedure

1. Set up an MBL/CBL system to collect data from a temperature probe at 6 second intervals for 100 data points.

2. Find and record the room temperature.

3. Insert the end of the probe into one thickness of the wool sock. Then place the sock-covered probe into a beaker of ice. Collect temperature data for 10 minutes.

4. View the graph of your data. If possible, print out the graph. Otherwise, plot the graph on graph paper.

5. Repeat steps 1–4 using a cotton sock and fresh ice.

Analysis

1. Analyze your data and determine which sock was the better insulator.

_____

_____

2. Summarize why these results are of importance to mammals.

_____

_____

_____

Copyright © by Holt, Rinehart and Winston. All rights reserved.

Data Lab

Comparing Gestation Periods

Background

If you have ever raised gerbils or hamsters, you know that they can produce several litters of young each year. That's because they have a very short gestation period compared to other mammals. Use the table below to find out more about gestation periods.

Gestation Periods in Mammals		
Mammal	**Gestation period**	**Offspring per pregnancy**
Vampire bat	210 days	1
Gerbil*	19–21 days	4–7
Human	about 265 days	1
Quarter horse	332–342 days	1
Black spider monkey	226–232 days	1
Grey squirrel	44 days usually	3
Rabbit*	about 31 days	3–6
Sperm whale	420–430 days	1
Arctic wolf	63 days	4–5

*More than two litters per year

Analysis

1. Critical Thinking
Recognizing Patterns State a generalization about the relationship between the length of the gestation period and the number of offspring per pregnancy.

_____

_____

2. Critical Thinking
Forming Hypotheses Propose a hypothesis to explain this relationship.

_____

_____

3. Recommend a way that the information in the table could be rearranged to show this relationship more clearly.

_____

_____

Copyright © by Holt, Rinehart and Winston. All rights reserved.

Recognizing Learned Behavior

Sow bugs must keep moist to survive. Follow the procedure below to see if sow bugs can learn to find moisture.

MATERIALS

• small wads of paper towel (one moist and one dry)

• T-maze made of two 6 cm (about 2.25 in.) pieces of 1.25 cm (0.5 in.) clear vinyl tubing

• sow bug

• blunt probe

Procedure

1. Place the moist paper wad in the open end of the left side of the T, and place the dry paper wad on the right side.

2. Place the sow bug at the bottom of the T. If it does not start to crawl, gently prod it with a blunt probe.

3. Observe what the sow bug does when it reaches the T section. Retrieve the sow bug and perform as many trials as time allows.

4. Keep a record of the results of each trial.

5. Using the same sow bug, repeat this procedure for three days.

Analysis

1. **Summarize** your sow bug's behavior, in writing or on a graph.

_____

2. **Describe** any trend in behavior that you observed.

_____

3. **Determine** if your sow bug modified its behavior through learning, using evidence to support your answer.

_____

_____

4. **Evaluate** the value of performing a final trial in which the T-maze contains two dry paper wads.

_____

_____

_____

Copyright © by Holt, Rinehart and Winston. All rights reserved.

Name _____ Class _____ Date _____

Observing Territorial Behavior in Crickets

The chirp of a male cricket attracts females and warns other males to stay away from his territory. You can study chirping behavior by observing crickets in an aquarium.

MATERIALS

- 5 male crickets, each marked with a different color
- 5 unmarked female crickets
- covered aquarium
- slice of apple and of potato
- small plastic jar
- 5 cm (2 in.) square of cardboard

Procedure

1. Place the crickets and food in an aquarium. Make two shelters by turning the plastic jar on its side and by folding the cardboard in half to form a tent-like structure.

2. You will be using the data table provided to record the behavior of the male crickets.

3. Observe the crickets for 10 minutes. Among the males, look for territorial (aggressive) behaviors—chirping, stroking others with antennae, pushing others away, etc.

4. For each observation of aggressive behavior, record the color of the aggressive male and where the behavior occurred—for example, next to the jar or the tent.

Data Table					
Cricket Behavior					
Cricket	Apple	Potato	Jar	Tent	Female
Blue					
Yellow					
Red					
Green					
White					

5. For each cricket, tally the number of times aggressive behavior was observed. Use a separate sheet of paper to make a list that ranks each cricket, placing the cricket with the highest tally on top.

6. Then tally the numbers for where the behaviors occurred. Rank the locations.

Copyright © by Holt, Rinehart and Winston. All rights reserved.

Analysis

1. **Critical Thinking**
   Analyzing Data Were any crickets more aggressive than the others?
   Give evidence to support your answer.

   _____

   _____

   _____

2. **Describe** the circumstances in which most aggressive behavior occurred.

   _____

   _____

   _____

3. **Propose** a reason to explain your answer to item 2.

   _____

   _____

   _____

4. **Critical Thinking**
   Forming Hypotheses For each aggressive behavior you observed, form
   a hypothesis that explains its function.

   _____

   _____

   _____

Copyright © by Holt, Rinehart and Winston. All rights reserved.

Quick Lab

Mapping the Valves in Veins

By applying pressure to your arm, you can locate the valves in the veins of your arm.

MATERIALS

• nontoxic felt-tip pen

Procedure

1. Have a classmate make a fist and extend his or her arm, with the hand palm up and slightly below elbow level. Locate a prominent vein on the inside of the forearm. Using one finger, press down on the vein at a point near the wrist to block the blood flow.

2. Gently place a second finger along the vein about 5 cm from the first finger (toward the elbow). Release the second finger, but not the first. The vein should refill partway. Mark this point, which indicates the location of a valve, with a pen. You may have to try more than one vein to locate a valve.

Analysis

1. **Identify** the direction blood flows in the vein you chose.

_____

_____

_____

2. **Propose** why the subject must make a fist and hold his or her arm slightly down.

_____

_____

_____

3. **Infer** what effect standing in one place for long periods of time might have on the veins in the legs.

_____

_____

_____

Copyright © by Holt, Rinehart and Winston. All rights reserved.

Math Lab

Calculating the Amount of Air Respired

Background

Most adults take in about 0.5 L of air with each breath. The normal breathing rate is about 8 to 15 breaths per minute.

Analysis

1. **Calculate** the volume of air in liters an adult breathes per minute if his or her breathing rate is 15 breaths per minute.

_____

_____

2. **Calculate** the volume of air in liters an adult breathes per hour if his or her breathing rate is 15 breaths per minute.

_____

_____

3. **Critical Thinking**
Inferring Conclusions The breathing rate of an infant is about 40 breaths per minute. Why might infants have higher respiratory rates than adults?

_____

_____

_____

_____

Copyright © by Holt, Rinehart and Winston. All rights reserved.

Modeling the Role of Bicarbonate in Homeostasis

You can use pH indicator paper, water, and baking soda to model the role of bicarbonate ions in maintaining blood pH levels in the presence of carbon dioxide.

MATERIALS

- two 250 mL beakers
- 250 mL distilled water
- 2.8 g baking soda
- glass stirring rod
- 4 strips of wide-range pH paper
- 2 drinking straws

Procedure

1. Label one beaker A and another B. Fill each beaker halfway with distilled water.
2. Add 1.4 g of baking soda to beaker B, and stir well.
3. Test and record the pH of the contents of each beaker.
4. Gently blow through a straw, into the water in beaker A. Test and record the pH of the resulting solution.
5. Repeat step 4 for beaker B.

Analysis

1. **Describe** what happened to the pH in the two beakers during the experiment.

   _____

   _____

   _____

2. **State** the chemical name for baking soda.

   _____

   _____

Copyright © by Holt, Rinehart and Winston. All rights reserved.

Modeling the Role of Bicarbonate in Homeostasis *continued*

3. Propose the chemical reaction that might have caused a change in pH in beaker A.

_____

_____

4. Summarize the effect the baking soda had on the pH of the solution in beaker B after blowing.

_____

_____

5. Critical Thinking
Applying Information Relate what happened in beaker B to what occurs in the bloodstream.

_____

_____

_____

_____

Copyright © by Holt, Rinehart and Winston. All rights reserved.

DATASHEET FOR IN-TEXT LAB

Modeling the Function of Bile

You can use a detergent and cooking oil to simulate the effect bile has on breaking up (emulsifying) fats as part of digestion.

MATERIALS

- two 250 mL beakers
- water
- cooking oil
- dish detergent
- stirring rod
- graduated cylinder

Procedure

1. Label one beaker *A* and one beaker *B*. Fill each beaker halfway with water.

2. Add 10 mL of the cooking oil to each beaker.

3. While stirring, slowly add 10 drops of dish detergent to beaker *B* only.

Analysis

1. Describe how oil reacts with the water.

_____

_____

2. Describe what happened to the oil when the dish detergent was added.

_____

_____

3. Compare the effect of dish detergent on oil with the effect of bile on fats.

_____

_____

4. Critical Thinking
Inferring Conclusions Do the detergents and bile increase or decrease the surface area of oil? In the case of bile, how does this help the digestive process?

_____

_____

_____

Copyright © by Holt, Rinehart and Winston. All rights reserved.

Name _____ Class _____ Date _____

DATASHEET FOR IN-TEXT LAB

Simulating Antigen Activity

Using simulated blood, you can see what happens when antigens encounter specific antibodies.

MATERIALS

- safety goggles
- disposable gloves
- lab apron
- 2 blood-typing trays

- simulated blood (types AB and O)
- simulated anti-A and anti-B blood-typing serums
- 4 toothpicks

Procedure

1. Put on safety goggles, disposable gloves, and a lab apron.

2. Place 3–4 drops of type AB simulated blood into each well in a clean blood-typing tray. **CAUTION: Use only simulated blood provided by your teacher.**

3. Add 3–4 drops of anti-A blood-typing serum to one well. Stir the mixture for 30 seconds using a toothpick. Add 3–4 drops of anti-B blood-typing serum to the other well. Use a new toothpick to stir the mixture. Look for clumps separating from the mixtures.

4. Repeat steps 2 and 3 using simulated type O blood.

5. Dispose of your materials according to your teacher's directions. Clean up your work area and wash your hands.

Analysis

1. **Determine** which blood type has antigens that are recognized by the blood-typing sera.

_____

2. **Evaluating Results** What does clumping of the blood mixtures indicate?

_____

3. **Predicting Outcomes** What would happen if you did the same experiment using type A blood and type B blood?

_____

_____

Copyright © by Holt, Rinehart and Winston. All rights reserved.

Name _____ Class _____ Date _____

Tracking the Spread of AIDS

Background

The graph below shows the total AIDS cases reported in the United States between 1996 and 2001. Use the graph to answer the questions that follow.

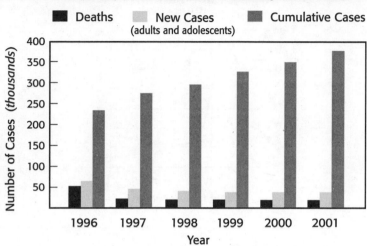

AIDS Cases in the United States, 1996–2001

Estimated data from Centers for Disease Control and Prevention

Analysis

1. Describe how the number of people with AIDS has changed since 1996.

_____

_____

2. Inferring Relationships Is the number of Americans infected with HIV most likely greater than or less than the number of people with AIDS? Explain why.

_____

_____

_____

3. Evaluating Data The graph indicates that the number of new AIDS cases reported each year has decreased since 1996. Suggest a possible reason for this decline.

_____

_____

_____

Copyright © by Holt, Rinehart and Winston. All rights reserved.

Name _____ Class _____ Date _____

DATASHEET FOR IN-TEXT LAB

Analyzing Changes During a Nerve Impulse

Background

The graph below illustrates changes that occur in the membrane potential of a neuron during an action potential. Use the graph to answer the following questions.

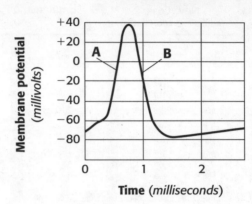

Action Potential

Analysis

1. Determine about how long an action potential lasts.

_____

2. State whether voltage-gated sodium channels are open or closed at point *A*.

_____

3. State whether voltage-gated potassium channels are open or closed at point *B*.

_____

4. Critical Thinking
Recognizing Relationships What causes the membrane potential to become less negative at point *A*?

_____

_____

5. Critical Thinking
Recognizing Relationships What causes the membrane potential to become more negative at point *B*?

_____

_____

Copyright © by Holt, Rinehart and Winston. All rights reserved.

Quick Lab) **DATASHEET FOR IN-TEXT LAB**

Demonstrating Your Blind Spot

The blind spot in your visual field corresponds to the site where the optic nerve exits the back of the eye. There are no photoreceptors at the site where the optic nerve exits. Use the procedure below to demonstrate your blind spot.

MATERIALS

unlined 3 × 5 index card

pencil

Procedure

1. On the index card, draw an X about 1 in. from the left side of the card. Draw an O about the same size 3 in. to the right of the X.

2. Hold your index card in front of you at arm's length. Close your right eye and stare at the O with your left eye. Slowly move the card toward you while continuing to stare at the O until the X disappears from view.

Analysis

1. **Name** the two kinds of photoreceptors found in the retina.

_____

_____

2. **Propose** why you cannot see images that fall on the site where the optic nerve exits the eye.

_____

_____

3. **Critical Thinking**
   Relating Concepts What is the relationship between the structure of the retina and the disappearance of the X on the index card?

_____

_____

_____

Copyright © by Holt, Rinehart and Winston. All rights reserved.

Math Lab

Analyzing Blood Glucose Regulation

Background

Eating simple sugars causes glucose to enter the bloodstream faster than eating complex carbohydrates or proteins. The rise in sugar levels triggers the secretion of insulin, which decreases blood glucose levels. On the graph, Meal #1 includes three waffles, a banana, and a glass of milk. Meal #2 includes two doughnuts and a 2 liter bottle of cola.

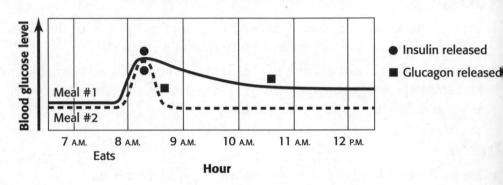

Different Meals and Blood Glucose Levels

● Insulin released

■ Glucagon released

Analysis

1. Identify which meal causes a faster rise in blood glucose.

_____

2. Critical Thinking
Inferring Determine which meal has complex carbohydrates and proteins that allow glucose to be released into the bloodstream more slowly.

_____

_____

3. Critical Thinking
Applying Hypoglycemic people have low blood glucose levels. They are often advised to eat six small meals a day containing little or no simple sugars. Why are these individuals given such advice?

_____

_____

_____

_____

Copyright © by Holt, Rinehart and Winston. All rights reserved.

Data Lab

DATASHEET FOR IN-TEXT LAB

Analyzing Hormone Secretions

Background

The ovarian and menstrual cycles are regulated by hormones secreted by the hypothalamus, the pituitary gland, and the ovaries. Feedback mechanisms play a major role in these cycles. Answer the following questions.

Analysis

1. Identify the hormones that are secreted in large amounts prior to ovulation.

_____

_____

_____

2. Describe the effect of estrogen production on the secretion of LH.

_____

_____

_____

3. Critical Thinking
   Analyzing Concepts What type of feedback mechanism causes a decrease in the secretion of LH and FSH during the luteal phase?

_____

4. Critical Thinking
   Analyzing Concepts What type of feedback mechanism causes the surge of LH secretion during the follicular phase?

_____

Copyright © by Holt, Rinehart and Winston. All rights reserved.